SYLVIA

SYLVIA

A Victorian Childhood

by

SYLVIA McCURDY

Eastland Press

Lavenham   Suffolk

1972

Published by
EASTLAND PRESS
S B N 903214 00 8

Printed in Great Britain by

THE LAVENHAM PRESS LIMITED

LAVENHAM   SUFFOLK

Contents

To a perfect mother and father

Introduction

THESE memories make no claim to be literature. They are the plain unvarnished account, more or less in chronological order, of events which made an impression on the mind of a child, a girl and a young woman. Many have faded. Such as remain have been recorded faithfully. The memories begin with the picture of a child walking up a hill and end when that child was approaching the hill of marriage.

1   *The Early Years*

I was born on April 5th, 1876, the third child, and elder daughter, of William and Anne Pinckard Stebbing. My father was the third of the eleven children of Dr. Henry Stebbing, D.D. and his wife, Mary, only daughter of Major Anderson, a Norfolk squire serving in one of His Majesty's Regiments of Foot. She must have possessed considerable strength of character since, well-brought up young lady as she was, she, aged eighteen, left her home early one morning and, attended only be a devoted maid-servant, drove to a village church and was there married to the handsome curate, aged twenty-three, on whom her mother had lately refused to bestow her hand. I have very little recollection of my grand-parents. My mother's mother died before I was born, her father when I was four years old, and as his death was followed by Irene (my sister), and I being dressed in black for six months, we did not think much of him. As my Stebbing grandfather always suggested that I should call a new doll, Sukey, a name I detested, preferring Violet or Eva, I did not think much of him, either. Though as he was known to his parishioners, and the patients at University College Hospital where he was Chaplain for many years, as the dear Doctor, I do him less than justice. Of my grandmother Stebbing I have one vivid memory. In extreme old age she was apt to turn day into night. One morning the whole brood of us were at the Parsonage. We saw her, clad in a dressing-gown, running up the long flight of stairs and gave chase—but could not catch her.

My two elder brothers, Will and Mark, Irene and I, were all born in Russell Square. On the south side of the Square: "You would not like a house on the north side of the Square: would you, my dear?" asked my unscientific father to my equally unscientific mother. "Oh, no, dear," agreed she. The House Agent had a house to let on the south side of the Square, so we were all born in a house into the

9

windows of which no glint of sun had ever penetrated. As we were probably fed on nothing but pap made by soaking bread baked in the oven in milk, for several months, we were, I imagine, then pale little specimens. But as the soot from the surrounding factory chimneys did penetrate, and the nurse complained that the white babies she took out came home looking like little sweeps and my father could not sleep when he came home from Printing House Square, for the noise of the horses and carts bringing up fruit and vegetables from the country to Covent Garden market, they decided to move to Hampstead. The house they chose was Heathland Lodge in the Vale of Health, below Spaniards Road. They chose it, my mother said, because it had a square entrance hall, paved with marble. All that I remember about it is a steep flight of stairs leading from the upper floor straight into the nursery, down which Irene fell and kept a permanent scar on her forehead. My youngest brother, Nigel, was born here in the middle of January 1879. My father told us that the snow lay so thick on the Heath that the cabman who drove him home each morning from *The Times* office could not drive right up to the house. As, wearily, he reached the door, he noticed a snowdrop in a sheltered spot and as he stooped to greet it, heard the thin wail of a newly-born child.

My very first memory is connected with the birth of this, my third brother. It is of walking up the hill to the church for his baptism. As my grandfather insisted on baptising all of us before the age of six weeks, since he believed that an unbaptised child went straight to Hell, I cannot have been more than two years and ten or eleven months old. Of the large garden I remember chiefly the potting-shed where we spent as much time as the disapproving eye of the nurse would allow us. We used the big pots as stools and the earth, called by the cockney gardener, dirt, as stuff to dig in. And then Irene and I were scolded because nurse said it was natural for boys to get dirty but little ladies should like to be clean. There was a big lawn and a kitchen-garden with fruit bushes. My father would sometimes take us there and pick us a few gooseberries. Of course it was forbidden for us to go there alone. But one day I took Nigel by the hand— and went there. I picked gooseberries and gave him some. "Where have you been?" asked nurse. "Nowhere," I said. Nigel, too young to be conscious of doing wrong, said "Sylvie ate the big gooseberries and gave me the little ones." I had my ears boxed for telling stories.

On Bank Holidays we were not taken out of the garden. We stood by the gate and said we were waiting to see Bank Holiday go by. I remember several walks in Hampstead. One day I was out with my mother and was swinging my arms, "You should not swing your arms," she said, "only postmen do that." So I never swung my arms again. Another day I was out with the nurse-maid. A soldier passed and said, "What a nice little girl." I do not think that children like having personal remarks made about them. I always tried to avoid that particular walk afterwards.

When Irene and I were about three and four years old, our parents asked a well-known water-colour artist to paint our portraits. It was quite amusing for a few minutes. She gave us flowers to hold and we wore pretty frocks but we very soon got tired of sitting still and the only way she could keep us from fidgetting was by promising each of us piece of chocolate if we kept still while she counted ten. The result in my case was quite good—the lady must have been thankful when the face was finished and she could put in the garden and the daisy chain and the muslin pinafore over a pink frock. I have the painting still and always wonder why she did not have my hair brushed before she painted it.

I was four years old when our-much loved Miss Carter joined the family circle to teach Will and Mark. I soon found that life in the schoolroom was more fun than that in the nursery, so crept in hoping to be unnoticed. "If you come in here," said Miss Carter, "you must learn to read." So, in spite of the dreary reading book I soon learnt to read. I can see that book still. It was called, "Reading without Tears" and was full of ugly little pictures. Another child soon joined the circle in the schoolroom. Lilian Scott, eldest child of Sir John Scott, Legal Advisor to the Khedive of Egypt. One day she told us she had a baby brother. "How big?" we asked. She put two slates together, one lengthwise, the other broadwise "That's how big," she said. The baby was Leslie Scott, later Sir Leslie Scott, Q.C. Another memory is of one night after Mark and I had been tucked up in bed. My mother came into the room and told us that Uncle Edward, who had just arrived from a visit to Paris, had brought us a present which was not to be opened till next morning. Uncle Edward then put a small packet near my bed. As soon as the door was shut Mark was out of bed and seized the parcel and tore it open. Inside was a little wooden box full of chocolate cigarettes, each one wrapped in thin paper like a real cigarette. Mark tipped the boxful onto my bed and as we could not see to take off the paper we ate them, paper and all, and I do not think I have ever eaten anything that tasted half as good. Another never-forgotten incident happened one day when I had been put for my rest in the spare-room. I was amusing myself in a tent I had made by fastening the counterpane to the rail at the head of the bed, when a great piece of the ceiling fell onto the bed. It missed me because I was screwed up on the pillow inside my tent. Hearing the noise some grown-ups rushed into the room. Now I should catch it for not resting properly, I thought. Not a bit of it. I was snatched up and kissed and petted. Another day I did not get off so easily. My father's great friend, Leonard Courtney, had come to play bowls on our lawn. I chose to show off by rolling about in front of them. Neither of them showed any sign of impatience but when nurse called me in I was smacked for being such a naughty rude little girl.

I was just over four when a whole week of adventure is still clear in my memory. I, and I alone of us five children, was taken by my parents to stay with my mother's father at his country house, Warley Elms in Essex. I don't think that the visit would have made so lasting an impression on me had it not been that a boy cousin aged six had also been staying there with his mother. He was the fifth son of my mother's elder sister, the wife of a Rector in Berkshire. As there were four little girls younger than himself, I imagine that the nurses were only too glad to be rid of him. I think that the only reason why I was the one chosen to accompany my parents was that I had not been very well. I remember that I was given a spoonful of nasty medicine every day after breakfast and that Eddie was ready to push a spoonful of marmalade into my mouth almost before I had swallowed the stuff. He lifted me up to see the eggs in the robin's nest in one of the great elms in the elm walk at the bottom of the garden. I waited impatiently for him to come out and play, while his mother gave him a reading lesson. He cried over his lesson but he enjoyed reading to me before we went to bed because I made no fuss when he left out the long words. Our grandfather, watching us from his bedroom window, would tap on the glass when Eddie ran on to the rosebeds after a ball. But as he never came into the garden Eddie did not seem to mind very much. To me he was perfect. Will and Mark were part of my every-day life; I could not imagine being without them. We played together and sometimes we squabbled. But Eddie was different. After this wonderful week Eddie and I did not meet for many years. Then one day his father, Uncle Oliver, brought Eddie and his four elder brothers to see us in Gloucester Terrace. Eddie was a gawky public schoolboy of about fifteen and I wondered what I had seen in him.

Between the ages of four and six I have few clear memories. Two children's parties I remember. One was on the first of May. It was my great friend, Bessy Kennedy's fifth birthday. We had tea in the garden. Her mother put a wreath of pink may on Bessy's chestnut curls. I thought she looked lovely and wished I could have a wreath on my hair when I was five. The other party was at the Rectory. The Rector, Mr. Bickersteth's two grown-up daughters were in charge of the tea-table. One of them asked Mark, "how many lumps of sugar do you like?" "Three, please." he said. She gave him two. I thought why did she ask him if she did not mean to give him what he asked for.

Soon after my sixth birthday we left Hampstead. The journey, night after night, to Printing House Square where my father was Assistant Editor to Mr. Delane, Editor of *The Times*, had become too great a strain on him. My mother's uncle, George Pinckard, said he would buy my parents a house in London. The house they chose was in Gloucester Terrace, near Kensington Gardens. It was not the more fashionable side of the Park but was said to be healthier. And this, with a view to bringing up five small children, decided them. It was a house built by an Englishman who had made a large fortune as a merchant in India. He had purchased the lease of a corner site from the Ecclesiastical Commissioners on which he undertook to build three houses. He built a large house for his own use in the centre with a small house on either side. The owner, Mr. Leech, died soon after he had moved in and my parents, thanks to Uncle George, bought the remainder of the lease for five thousand pounds. It had over fifty years to run. I remember asking what would happen to all of us when the lease came to an end.

I have a clear memory of arriving at the house. My parents, with the maids and Will and Mark arrived first, leaving the two nurses, Irene, Nigel and me to come when the house was straight. It was all so immense. Mark stood at the top of the first flight of stairs and called to me to come up. I ventured up a few steps, and then, in spite of his encouragement, went down again. All the rooms were large. The drawing-room was forty feet long and nineteen feet high with naked cherubs running all round the domed edge of the ceiling. It had a wide bay window at one end of the room and two other windows so high that the effort of opening them at the top was beyond a house-maid's strength, and I never remember to have seen them opened. My father's library was behind the front portion of the drawing-room and faced Cleveland Terrace. It was as high as the drawing-room so my parents had it cut in two. The lower half was the library and the top half my parents' bedroom and dressing-room with a tiny staircase which led, I was told, though I never ventured up, into a lavatory. My father never used any of the other lavatories though there were three others in the house. There was only one bathroom and one cold water tap nearly at the top of the house. My parents and visitors had hip-baths in their bed and dressing-rooms with huge brass hot-water jugs, all of which had to be filled in the kitchen and carried up all those stairs. The library had a great fascination for us, partly because it held so many amusing things. In the middle was a round table which swivelled round and had innumerable little drawers under the top, each with different things in it. Pens and pencils and boxes of nibs and all sorts of writing paper and one drawer full of ivory paper-knives. We never knew what to get for my father's birthday so we clubbed together and bought him an ivory paper-knife. We often saw my mother cutting the edges of new books with a paper-knife and there was nothing else he needed. Then there was the window with a window-box outside it, glazed in to keep out the noise of carriages and hansoms rattling down the street. People in those days must have been very susceptible to noise as I can remember several occasions when I saw straw laid down in the street and being told that someone in a house nearby was ill. I thought it must be a wonderful thing to happen to anyone. There was always a bunch of everlasting flowers in the middle of the round table. This was provided for Mr. Punch, the half Persian tabby-cat who ate one after his breakfast every morning. My father's repeater watch ended the show. It not only told the hour but also the number of quarters past the hour. It was given to him after Mr. Delane's death as it was the watch he had always worn. After his death my father no longer went to *The Times*' office but worked at home, writing the first leading articles for *The Times*. He also wrote book reviews for *The Spectator* and other papers. It was very hard work and he was glad when *The Times* increased his salary on condition that he should only write for them.

It was probably between leaving Hampstead and going to school, that I experienced a strange sensation. Although I can remember it as a fact, it is difficult to describe. It was as though I had no longer any bodily presence. As though I had vanished into 'thin air'. It was not at all an unpleasant sensation. In fact, as it was fading, I tried, without success, to prolong it. How long it lasted I have no idea, nor of how often I experienced it. As I never mentioned it to anyone I do not know if it is a common sensation. Perhaps the best way to describe it is of a fading away.

It was not long after we moved to Gloucester Terrace that we made a great discovery. There was a lavatory and wash-basin just opposite the stairs down to the kitchen and beyond them a bolted door. The

14

bolts were very rusty and we could not move them. Where does it lead to? We pestered Jane until at last she consented to pull back the bolts. The door opened onto a steep flight of cobwebby stone steps. At the end of them was a short passage and that led, wonder of wonders! into a huge garden. We raced back up the steps, shouting at the tops of our voices, Mother! Mother! She hurried out of the dining room convinced that one of us must be badly hurt. We dragged her down the steps and into the garden. She was as astonished as we had been. Not a word of it had been said by the house-agent to my parents. The two acre garden was open to our block of Gloucester Terrace, to Gloucester Gardens on our side of Bishop's Road and to Cleveland Terrace as far as the two shops and the public-house which led to Porchester Terrace. This last road fascinated us. The houses were very large with wide gates through which no one seemed to go in or out. In the largest house of all William Whiteley lived. Occasionally the gate would be opened and out would come one of his sons on horseback, wearing beautiful white riding breeches. There were many stories of Mr. Whiteley in those days: it was said he engaged his assistants without a character and dismissed them at a moment's notice, and there was the mystery of the burning down of his shops until no insurance company would insure them.

It must have been soon after we left Hampstead that I became aware of the large number of people to whom I was expected to pay special attention because they were relations; I had no choice in the matter. They were uncles and aunts if old, cousins if young. My mother had very few of these special people. She was the youngest of a family of three girls. The eldest married a parson in Berkshire and bore him, without, I imagine, much thankfulness on his part, eleven children. She was devoted to her parish and seldom left it. Her second sister had married a younger brother of my father. Not a very harmonious arrangement and we did not meet our seven cousins until later in life. Of my father's brothers and sisters we saw a great deal. His eldest brother, John, was interesting but feckless. He was clever but had tastes beyond his means. He used to complain that, had he been an only child he would have done very well. He left Cambridge in debt and became tutor to various sprigs of the aristocracy. He wrote a long poem on "The Wandering Jew", and as far as I know, wrote nothing else. As he was a bachelor he spent all the anniversaries in our cheerful and hospitable house. He had a passion for telling us long tales of knights and dragons and damsels in distress and sent the boys down into the hall to collect walking-sticks to make the story more

15

alive. They were exciting tales but he would keep stopping to explain the meaning of a word. We did not mind a scrap if we did not know the word, all we wanted was to hear what happened at the end.

The next uncle was Tom. His wife, Aunt Milly, was great fun. Irene and I loved Uncle Tom but to the boys he was apt to be rather sarcastic. They had no children but a host of devoted nephews and nieces on both sides of the family, even if Uncle Tom did occasionally try to take us down a peg or two. In later years I remember Aunt Milly saying, "If you had not been such nice children you would have been utterly spoilt." Uncle Tom had, like many scientists, a love of making puns. This amused us children, particularly because our mother saw no fun in them. When he made one we looked out of the corners of our eyes at Aunt Milly, who, good wife that she was, always smiled. Then at our mother who tried to look as if she had not heard. My father said that when he went to a Royal Society Dinner as the guest of his brother puns and jokes would pop out all along the table like bubbles on a glass of champagne.

Irene and I often spent our half-term holiday with them at Ephraim Lodge, on the Common, Tunbridge Wells. A precise ritual was followed on the Sunday. There were always sausages for breakfast. Then the pot-plants, a goodly array as there was no garden, were watered. Then the walk to the Church on Rusthall Common. Uncle Tom read the lessons. Though forbidden to preach owing to his advanced Darwinian theories he was still an ordained member of the Church of England and had been a very popular preacher in Torquay. He was very human. I remember his remarking how pleasant it was to see in the rather distant pew where Aunt Milly always sat, the cherry-coloured ribbons in our hats. He wondered why so many women thought it Sabbatical to wear dull clothes on a Sunday. After early dinner the two maids were given their choice of a book to read before going out for the rest of the day. "Oh! please, Mum, one of Miss Grace's." I always wondered whether the choice were guided by a desire to please, or because they really liked Aunt Grace's books. Punctually at nine o'clock Aunt Milly went down to the back-door to let in the two maids who always arrived at the same instant. I knew these two maids well. Clara, the cook, was with them for forty years. The house-parlour maids only left to be married and then others gladly took their places.

My father's youngest surviving brother, Edward, lived in Gower Street with his wife, Fanny and their eight children. The four boys and their eldest sister were properly educated, two of the boys at University College School and two at St. Paul's. But the three younger girls had no schooling beyond that given them by an ancient German governess who came for a few hours each morning. I presume that the School Board did not function in the 1880s or one of their Inspectors would have noticed three pale little faces, gazing, day after day, out of the dining-room window, on the chance of seeing a passer-by. Uncle Edward, a lively young man who loved music and dancing, had left the rather severe atmosphere of the Parsonage where such delights were not so much frowned upon, as ignored, at the age of twenty-three. He soon married a willowy lady a few years his senior and eked out a meagre living as a junior Civil Servant, by taking pupils and becoming Secretary to the Thames Rowing Club. To Uncle John, Edward never quite grew up. I remember his muttering, "Fancy listening to that chit," when my father asked his younger brother's opinion on some matter. To me they were all old men. John's chief complaint was that he was not an only child. Life could then have been so much easier as all the attention would have been lavished on him alone.

Although my mother's sisters, with their large families, were in no way remarkable she had two maiden aunts of considerable interest. Aunt Jane lived at Worthing. One day while we were at Lancing my mother took Irene and me to see her. At the time she must have been in her eighties. After we left we had for some reason to return to the house and were amused to see Aunt Jane arm-in-arm with an old gentleman on their way down to the sea. This, her maid told us, was their regular habit. It was this Aunt Jane who visited her six nieces and their families not very long before her death. Each niece gave her, in their several ways, their most favoured treatment. Aunt Jane went home and noted, as a codicil to her last Will and Testament, that as all her nieces were so comfortably off, she bequeathed the whole of her property to a Home for the Indigent Poor. Aunt Rachel lived with two devoted maids in a house in Tavistock Square. I remember the sitting-room well and Aunt Rachel, in a lace cap, still beautiful. My mother told us that when she was young she was so lovely and amusing that many men fell in love with her, but if one of them ventured too near she would box his ears. We loved her as she always gave us little chocolate bottles with names of French wines on them. One day my father took us to visit her. As we were leaving she said, "They must have their wine." "They don't drink wine," began my father. She paid no attention and brought out her chocolate bottles. Aunt Rachel divided her property equally among her six nieces.

In my youth the conditions in which hard-working, respectable people were forced to bring up their families, were appalling. It was not only in London and other great cities that such squalor was permitted. Wages in agricultural districts were so low that food and clothing were inadequate. When I was growing up eighteen shillings a week was the normal wage. The wives added to this working by in the fields and in the big houses occasionally, but the children looked thin and pale. At fourteen or fifteen the daughters went into service. Those with a taste for sewing, and a liking for small children, became nursery-maid and often stayed long enough in the family to become a head-nurse and her mistress's confidante, while the kitchen-maid hoped to learn enough from the cook to qualify her to become a cook-general or cook. A great number of these under-fed little girls, who were fortunate enough to serve under a kindly head servant, blossomed into comely young women who probably married a fellow servant or one of the lads who carried the meat or groceries down the area steps to the back door. He might well find the country-bred girl less exacting than the pert town-bred maiden. This was as well for it used to be said that three generations of city-bred couples produced progeny who were weakly, either mentally or physically. But neither town nor country-folk seem to have been taught in those days any rules of hygiene. I never saw a country cottage where the windows were kept open, even by day. The night air was thought to be unwholesome. I have seen quite good-looking cottages where the windows were not made to open. Our parents, on the contrary, thought so highly of fresh air that they took us to the sea for a fortnight in the Easter holidays and for six weeks to the country in the summer. We could never go far afield because my father had to be near enough to town to get the subject for next day's leading article down by the morning train and the finished article back by the last train. We did not care much for the Easter holidays. It was too cold to bathe and the landlords at the seaside lodgings never approved of our knocking balls against the sitting-room walls. We were glad to be home again in spite of our mother's insistence that we should swallow a dose of castor-oil the first evening. On one such occasion Miss Carter was given the unpleasant task of getting us to take it. We all cried. Mark said he wouldn't take it unless everybody left the room. Then Mark opened the window and threw the horrible stuff out. I think that was the last time it was given us. In the summer we took a house big enough for us five children, several maids, our parents and the guinea-pigs. A good garden was essential and here we ran wild. I think that children of my day who were brought up in London under the correct eyes of nurses and governesses, had their spirits so firmly brought under control, that when they were let loose in the country their spirits were apt to run riot. How delightful it was to do as we chose. Not to wear gloves or hats. We were, like Alexander Selkirk, monarch of all we surveyed. We burst through hedges, we climbed the trees. We fished the ponds and even the ditches. We brought back, in time for our parents' breakfast, sticklebacks and Millers' Thumbs. These our devoted cook fried and our still more devoted parents ate, while we stood watching them savouring each muddy morsel they put into their mouths. Years later my mother confessed how revolting these little fish had been. And, Oh; the things you could buy in the one tiny general shop. Penny ices; stick-jaw called chew-girls; chew, a very thin slab of toffee wrapped in paper; Jumbo's chains and telegraph wires made of liquorice. We had collected a good store of these for a future feast and put them on the dining-room mantelpiece. On our return from some expedition they had gone! We knew our mother disapproved of them. We did not speak of our loss, neither did she. On the other hand she never seemed to tire of peeling us six-a-penny pears and cutting us slices of melon to ward off the pangs of hunger before lunch-time. Her theory was that fruit might be eaten before a meal, but never sweets or cakes. Altogether this place was perfect from a child's point of view. It was both seaside and country: and such glorious country. Great wide downs on which you could walk for miles without seeing another soul. And the seaside, just a sandy shore with two or three huts for hire and a few old coast-guards on watch so that there was no need for grown-ups to get panicky if the sea were rough. The village was cut in two by a railway line, so that the few summer visitors seldom came to the countryside. The house our parents took was on the downs side of the track. We only crossed it in the mornings for a bathe and a visit to the little shop. The afternoons we spent in the garden, jumping over and playing hide and seek among the bushes. They must have needed a good deal of tying up when we left. After tea when my father's article for *The Times* had been entrusted to the engine driver to be posted when he got to London, we all went for walks on the downs. By this time our spirits had cooled off, for our day started early. I think Jane may have been on holiday. Certainly there was no one to force us to wait in bed till we were called. As soon as we heard the boys stirring, Irene and I were out of bed and throwing on our clothes. Vest, knickers and a sailor suit. Off with pails and fishing rods to that delectable land between sea and farmland where little eels lived in the rivulets. I was not as useful to the boys as Irene was. She did not mind baiting their hooks with bits of worm. I detested it, so spent my time walking round the hedges, watching the dewdrops on the spiders' webs sparkle in the rising sun. The land belonged to a farmer whose son disapproved of us. So we had to get down to the marshland before he was up in the morning. One day we stayed out too long. We saw the farm door open and our enemy come out. He saw us and began to run. We were just in time to escape him, but had to leave our catch behind. Most of the farmers were friendly and let us play in their farmyards where we chased the baby pigs and were chased by the sow. This delightful place was called Lancing.

2   *The Family Entertains*

Though we enjoyed the holidays we managed to get plenty of fun in London after lessons were over. When Will and Mark were back from Mr. Wilkinson's (a day preparatory school in Orme Square) and Miss Carter had gone after tea, we had the schoolroom to ourselves. The schoolroom maid had cleared away the tea things and was thankful to have done with us till she brought in our meagre supper of a glass of milk and a small helping of neat's foot jelly. More nourishing, my mother said, than calf's foot jelly.

There could have been no more glorious playground than that tall, spacious house in Gloucester Terrace. In some ways we were singularly happy in our home life. To begin with we were just the right size. We were also close together. Will, the eldest, was only five and three-quarters years than Nigel, the youngest. We were not so small a family that we had not enough playfellows, nor so large that the younger ones were kept in the nursery under the strict supervision of the nurse, and saw little of their parents. My mother gave up keeping a nurse when we left Hampstead. Jane, the nursery-maid, became schoolroom maid. Her chief duty was to put us to bed and get us up in the morning and bring up our meals. Otherwise she left us much to ourselves, and left to ourselves we played wonderful games. When we grew tired of playing Old Witch and I wanted a change because I always had to be Old Witch, we would go up to the attic playroom. Here we had an enormous rocking-horse, big enough to take all five of us at once. Two on his back, one on either end and one underneath. My mother had had a trapeze hung from a beam in the ceiling and on this I managed to let go with one hand just long enough to write my name, letter by letter in the dust on the ceiling. And the little bamboo house that we could all just squeeze into which may have been sent from Jamaica as my parents had friends there who brought us delicious pieces of sugar-cane. There was another attic next to our playroom with a large chest in it. Here I found an old book and delved in it. Henceforth I received much kudos from the rest of us for scraps of information, chiefly on the subject of beds. That was all I had time to gather for it mysteriously disappeared after my first perusal of it or I am sure I should have gone on reading it. It was called "Advice to a Young Matron" or some such title. We always played in a gang together so it was a great shock when one evening a schoolfriend of Will's, following him up to the playroom, said, "Do we have to have that lot with us?" We did not wait for Will's answer but turned and slunk back to the schoolroom.

It was a glorious house for games. When it happened that our parents were out and the maids were busy in their sitting-room in the basement, we would play Hide and Seek, all over the house—except in our parents' bedroom and the library. The drawing-room was our paradise with the big curtained windows and huge sofas and chairs with chintz covers down to the floor. Best of all were the stairs for tobogganing. In the playroom were a couple of short benches. These, turned upside down, were ideal for the purpose. Each took two of us. We piled all the drawing-room cushions at the foot of the stairs, leading from the half-landing outside our parents' bedroom down to the wide landing outside the drawing-room, and then let the benches go, one after the other. Strange to say I never remember any of us being seriously hurt. Another favourite game was sliding down the banisters. Our parents had been aware that we were likely to indulge in this pastime so they had had brass rails fitted on top of the wooden ones on all the upper staircases. But, luckily for us, because of the look of the thing, only brass knobs had been put at intervals on the rails from the drawing-room floor to the ground-floor. And we got very expert at lifting a leg over each knob as we came to it and scarcely slackening our pace. Of course we had to keep our ears wide open for any sound from the kitchen floor. For Martha, the large Welsh housemaid, had a heavy hand when she chose to use it. Luckily her elastic-sided boots squeaked and before she had climbed up the stone stairs from the kitchen and up the stairs from the dining-room floor we had thrown all the cushions back onto the sofas and chairs, pulled the toboggans up into the playroom and while she was tidying up the drawing-room, slipped down into the schoolroom where, it being Jane's domain, even Martha could not follow us. Not that Jane had much authority over us. Years later when Irene and I were staying at a friend's house in Abingdon where Jane was then housemaid, I asked her if the half-dozen pugs in the house were easier to manage than we had been. "Far easier," she said—"You were all tiresome children, but that Master Markie, he was the worst of all. He would get the other side of the table where I couldn't get at him and call out, 'Idiot, idiot'''.

We often went to tea with friends who lived very near us. They, too, had access to the same gardens. Our friends' mother was a widow. Her unmarried sister lived with her. One night they sat up reading until about eleven o'clock. Then they put the guard in front of the fire, shook up the cushions and went to the door. The maids had locked it. They went to the french window which led to the garden staircase and called to the man who patrolled the gardens every night. They asked him to go round to the front door and ring the upstairs bell which hung outside the maids' bedrooms. But the maids had forgotten to alter the wires to make the bell ring upstairs instead of in the basement. So no amount of ringing woke the maids and their mistresses were weary and cold when at seven o'clock next morning the parlourmaid unlocked the door. The three children of this house and I, but not Irene, all caught scarlet fever from milk drunk in their house. One afternoon I felt hot and miserable. Both Miss Carter and Madame Princep (our French governess) were in the school-room. Madame said, "I should like to look at her stomach." I was sure that Miss Carter would not allow me to be subjected to such an indignity. Then my mother came and sent for the doctor and I was put to bed with scarlet fever. A whole floor with its four bedrooms was given up to me. A curtain was hung over the passage leading to them and a hospital-nurse was engaged. At first I resented her, and when she proceeded to rub me all over with vaseline I loathed her. But she was a charming young woman and very soon I was calling her "Nobody" and listening to her stories; including the *Mistletoe Bough* which gave me the slight claustrophobia from which I still suffer. My mother refused to be entirely kept away from me and visited me for a few minutes every morning. After four weeks she took me to Hastings for a fortnight. A wonderful fortnight in a little old terrace house in the Old Town facing the sea and the harbour where the fishermen mended their nets. Every morning we bought fish from the fishwives standing in the centre of the circular fish-market. Here, now, is a space where one may stand in safety from the motorcars. Then, small basin in hand, we would walk down Robertson Street and buy Devonshire cream from the dairy. The highlight of the fortnight was a visit—my first—to a pantomime, *Little Red Riding Hood* on the Hastings Pier.

There was a great gale on Saturday night and next morning huge waves broke over the foreshore and up the little narrow streets. Well-dressed ladies went to church in boats. Such an adventure, I thought, might make going to even a dreary service worth while, and our services at home were very dreary. Our Vicar was very old and his sermons very long.

I was nine years old and our landlady's children were much younger, so I cut them out paper dolls with paper dresses. It was fun being looked up to. It made me feel almost grown up. It took some time to get used to being one of five again after being the one spoilt darling for so long.

Miss Carter who, as a girl of nineteen, had come to us to teach Will and Mark to read and write, remained as our governess for seven or eight years. While our parents went abroad for their annual spring holiday Miss Carter stayed in the house to look after us. To her we all, particularly we three younger ones, owe a great debt of gratitude— she taught us to love reading in a wide range of literature. While we lay flat on our backs on the hard cork-carpeted schoolroom floor, after lunch, she read to us endlessly. Many of Dickens' novels—her favourite being, I remember, *Bleak House*—some of Scott, including *Tales of a Grandfather*, *Tanglewood Tales* and *Lamb's Tales from Shakespeare*. As well as, on the lighter side, the two *Alices*, Harrison Ainsworth's novels and stories by Edgar Allan Poe. The last two authors, rather too creepy for young children perhaps, but we all, governess included, enjoyed them. There was one book which we loved beyond all others—stories from Spenser's *Faerie Queene*. They were, I think, put into modern English by Mrs. Haweis, wife of a very popular preacher of my youth. He used to get so excited in the pulpit that he seemed to be in peril of flinging himself headlong into the laps of the congregation. Another book which I used to read at the beginning of every holiday was *Castle Blair* by Flora Shaw.

We loved our walks with Miss Carter in Kensington Gardens and Hyde Park. There were lambs to be seen in the spring. The ewes had been driven into Hyde Park from the country. Not such a long journey in those days. Later there was sheep-shearing. Such sorry-looking creatures when it was over: even the lambs looked distressed. Then

24

in the hot summer days there were small naked urchins dodging the Park keepers and tumbling about in the Long Water in Kensington Gardens. I remember one of these keepers gathering up the little bundles of clothes and walking off with them. Though we begged to stay and see what happened next we were dragged off for our tea.

One afternoon we were shocked into silence. We were walking inside the Park, near Hyde Park Gate, when we noticed a little group of people standing on the pavement on the further side of the road outside the park. An open barouche drove along the road. In it sat Queen Victoria with Princess Beatrice by her side. As it passed them the little knot of people on the pavement hissed. It was not a loud sound, but unmistakable. We looked at Miss Carter in awed silence. "I think," she said, "that the people do not like the Queen spending so much time in Scotland."

Two other occasions are connected with Queen Victoria. On only one of them did I actually see her. At her Golden Jubilee in 1887 my father took Irene, Nigel and me to see the Illuminations. We started by underground from Bishop's Road to Marble Arch. Then we walked along Oxford Street, down Regent Street and along Piccadilly as far as St. James's Street. Then, best of all to our eyes, we saw the clubs in Pall Mall. As if this were not enough for our young legs, we went east, through ever-thickening crowds, to the Bank of England and St. Paul's. Here, for some reason, a gate had been closed across a road. My father had to protect us three small children from the pressure of the crowds. Those in front suddenly stopped by the unexpected barrier and those behind who had not seen the temporary gate trying to push forward. Luckily the mass of people was too dense for anyone to fall.

None of the streets were decorated as units then. But for sheer brilliance as seen by the eyes of a child, no illuminations have ever equalled those of Queen Victoria's Golden Jubilee, particularly those on the Clubs. On the way home my father went into the Athenaeum and was distressed that he was not allowed to take us beyond the hall, nor to give us a glass of lemonade.

Irene and I saw the Diamond Jubilee Procession in 1897 from seats erected in front of the National Gallery for the Keeper of the National Gallery, Mr. Eastlake, and his friends. A magnificent position, as we had such a long view. Beneath our seats were those allotted to the

Peers of the Realm and their relations. Among them we noticed a friend, Nigel Playfair. I remember that at the next dance we were both at, he asked me to which branch of the peerage we belonged. There can have been no site in the whole of London better suited to display a procession than that in front of the National Gallery. As far as the sight could reach, beyond the fountains in Trafalgar Square, sparkling in the sun that always greeted Queen Victoria, watched by the eye of Nelson on his column, came the massed regimental bands. At last came the moment we had longed for. The open carriage in which sat the Queen. It was drawn by six superb horses. There may have been royal ladies in the carriage with her, but I had no eyes for anyone but the Queen. Small, dumpy, supremely regal, dressed in black, the older she grew the more beloved she seemed to become. The cushions had been fitted with springs so that Her Majesty might acknowledge the cheers of her people without undue exertion. Her grandson, Kaiser Wilhelm II of Prussia, the Czar of all the Russias, all the crowned heads of Europe were in the procession, many of them, including the Prince of Wales, on horseback near Her Majesty's state carriage. When the last sound of the bands had died away we were entertained to luncheon by the Keeper and his wife. The sight that remains most vividly in my memory is of that little figure in deep black, looking so happy and moved by the evident love of her people.

Although Queen Victoria in her old age inspired a great deal of affection, she had not escaped criticism in the handling of the Prince of Wales. The duties of kingship, even in those days, needed learning. The Queen gave her son no opportunity of learning them. He had many good qualities which appealed to the English taste. He was a sportsman and loved boisterous fun, but he was not the least like his father. And this fact probably upset his mother so that she gave him no credit for the gifts he had. He was sent to Oxford and Cambridge, each for one year. While at one of them he planned a night out in London, but somehow the Queen got wind of it. When the train arrived in London the Prince was accosted by a footman who informed him that a carriage was waiting to drive him to Buckingham Palace. The Prince took the next train back to his Alma Mater. Every year the Prince spent a weekend at a great house in Leatherhead for the pheasant shooting. A very old friend of mine in Southwark told me that her father was brother to the Head Game-keeper at the great house. Sometimes she and her brothers and sisters were invited to stay in the servants' quarters. They were allowed to watch the departure of the Royal guest from the dormer windows at the top of the house. The

Leatherhead tradesmen were warned not to have their horses and carts out on the morning the Prince left, because he drove his gig at a great pace along the narrow, twisting streets of the town.

Christmas was the only day on which we sat up to dinner. It was not the custom in our house to hang up stockings for Santa Claus to fill. The first excitement was the coming of the postman at breakfast time. Then it was a race between us and the parlourmaid to get to the front door. The postman did not wait for the door to be opened but went on pushing bundle after bundle through the letter-box. We bore them to the schoolroom and began to sort them out. As both cards and postage were so cheap all our cousins and friends sent them to all of us. Then we joined our parents in the dining-room for our presents. Usually we had one big present for all of us. I remember two of these: a cooking-stove, heated by methylated spirit and big enough to cook a real meal, and a printing press. I am afraid we—certainly the boys—looked on this as another method of instruction. Then came church and on our return we sniffed up the delicious smell of roasting goose, which the maids were having for their Christmas dinner, while we were to have, as usual, boiled beef. After tea came Snapdragons. A huge china dish half full of raisins was put on the schoolroom table, brandy was poured onto them and set alight. You hated the taste of brandy and you hated to get your fingers burnt, but you had to pretend to pull the raisins out of the flames for fear that Uncle Tom would think you a coward. At last it was dinner time and you wanted to taste everything. Soup and turkey with all the trimmings, cranberry sauce and bread sauce and sausages and sprouts. Best of all—dessert. Almonds and raisins and dates and plums. Your tummy was so full it ached. "Sylvia," said my mother, "You have eaten too much." And you burst into tears. And kind Uncle Edward said, "Oh no," and offered you a bit of dry biscuit. Soon you were all right again and everyone went into the drawing-room to watch Blind Man's Buff. My father was always Blind Man and he was not blind-folded. He used to pretend he couldn't see you and when he caught one of you he said you were someone else. And how fast he could run if he meant to catch you. It was our favourite game and we played it every Christmas and birthday until my mother said it must stop as it was too exhausting for father. When at last bedtime came I meant to stay awake to hear the Waits singing, but I never heard them.

3 Sundays, Dinner Parties and At Homes

Twice a year my parents gave three dinner-parties. Three in the winter and three in the Season. To my mother, shy and reserved, these functions must have been very burdensome, but to my father a source of enjoyment. A list of guests, eighteen for each party, would be drawn up. When some guests were unable to accept, others would be put in their place. I remember one occasion when my mother, expecting some refusals, had twenty-two acceptances and had to call in a carpenter to add a piece of deal to the end of the mahogany table. I remember a time when my mother needed all her power of self-control at one of these dinners. She was very fond of blue china. Only for a dinner-party were the blue plates used. A young manservant was carrying up the kitchen stairs eighteen of these plates when he slipped. The whole trayful crashed to the ground. The noise was of course heard in the dining-room! one voice only did not falter—my mother's.

Before they went to boarding school Will and Mark used to lie in wait, just inside the schoolroom door, armed with plate and spoon ready to pounce on the maids, but never on the tall, imposing hired waitresses, as they left the dining-room, so as to snatch what they could of the delicious dishes. "Now, master Markie, that dish hasn't been touched. It's to be left for tomorrow," the under-parlourmaid would plead. The guests, too, had their difficult moments. Mr. Fred Walker, High Master of St. Paul's and Dr. Jex-Blake, lately Headmaster of Rugby, and now Dean of Wells, were sitting not far from one another. To my father's consternation Mr. Walker, a layman, said in his booming voice, "If a headmaster in Holy Orders is a success he's made a Bishop, if a failure, a Dean."

They were elaborate and expensive affairs, these dinner-parties. Even if the cooks were capable of cooking the whole meal, the ingredients were expensive. The two waitresses, apart from their wages, expected the best of food and drink for their supper. My mother's dinners were not the lengthiest, but they started with thick and clear soup, then fish followed by a brown and a white entrée. Then a joint, probably saddle of mutton; game according to season or chicken finished the solid part of the meal. It ended with a creamy sweet and ices. Peoples' appetites must have been larger in those days for some guests even toyed with a few hothouse grapes or a peach to end up with. Then my father opened the door for the ladies to leave the dining-room and he returned to occupy the chair lately occupied by my mother. Sherry was served with the fish, champagne with the rest of the dinner, liqueurs with the dessert. My mother told me that at a dinner-party soon after she was married an old gentleman said to her: "You can take liqueurs now that you are married, Mrs. Stebbing." While the gentlemen in the dining-room drank coffee and port, the ladies in the drawing-room drank coffee and discussed their children and domestics. I think that one of the reasons why so many women now take an intelligent interest in public affairs is that domestics can no longer engage their attention.

Irene and I used to enjoy helping or hindering my mother in dressing for these parties. The house-maid did the tying or buttoning-up processes but we chose the ornaments most suitable for the dress. One night there came a knocking on the bedroom door. Martha met a panic-stricken kitchen-maid. "The cook has not turned up," she said. Sometimes if the cooks were not very efficient my mother would engage the proprietor of a restaurant in Notting Hill to come and cook the more elaborate of the dishes. "Take a cab," she told the kitchen-maid, "drive to the restaurant and bring the man straight back with you." Within half an hour the apologetic cook with such of his dishes he had ready in his own kitchen was in our kitchen cooking for the eighteen guests. Dinner was half an hour late but my father had such a good tale to tell that everyone was happy.

In another respect, though I doubt our being aware of it, we had a great deal to be thankful for in our parents. There was none of the stiffness between parents and children that is emphasized in many of the biographies of that day. In an age before wireless or television, people were more dependent on their own resources for entertainment. Girls were expected to play the piano or to sing after a dinner-party. And children were trained at a very early age to recite poetry on their mothers' "At Home" days. Our mother was too wise to expect us to do any such thing. It was an age, too, of good conversation. My father had the power, not only of talking brilliantly himself, but of getting other people to talk. It was also the age of anecdote and several of my father's college friends, when staying with us, would keep the whole dinner table amused by anecdotes. It is not now considered to be the highest form of conversation, but at least it was a pleasant form of family entertainment. Canon Wace, then Principal of King's College in the Strand, and later Dean of Canterbury, was the finest exponent of anecdotage I have met, closely followed by Dr. Henry Daniel, Provost of my father's old college, Worcester.

Many hostesses provided an entertainer at an afternoon or evening "At Home". Corney Graine was a favourite at such parties. He arrived at dinner-time at a big house where he was to recite. He was shown into the servants' hall and given supper. After supper he gave a performance to the domestics. The master of the house rang for the butler and told him to show Mr. Corney Graine up the drawing-room. "Tell your master that where I dine I recite," he told the butler. And left the house.

Canon Ainger, Master of the Temple Church, was another fine entertainer. He read Dickens beautifully. He was very fond of children and liked to be asked to their parties. Having, as he thought, been asked to one of these, when the door was opened for him he went in on his hands and knees, growling like a bear. But it was a grown-up party.

Apart from real experts like these, it was usual for boys and girls to help entertain their parents' guests. I do not speak from personal experience as we were, as a family, too dumb to sing, play or recite, but our friends did. "Do give us a little piece on the piano." Or, "Sing us one of your charming songs." Played or sang they never so badly, one sat through it, being thankful that our mother's ear was too good to allow us to perform. These performances took place while the male members of the party were still lingering over their gossip and port.

My mother was a complete contrast to my father. She was, to begin with, a listener not a talker. I have a pleasant picture of them in old age, she with eyes fixed upon his face while he reads from one of his translations of Latin or Greek poems. He used to say that his hands were useless—and, indeed, I never saw him drive in a nail or cut a slice of bread. To counterbalance this my mother's hands were of the cleverest. I possess many volumes of her flower drawings, botanically correct in every detail. My father enjoyed long walks and was always on the lookout for specimens to tuck into the lining of his felt hat.

When there were no more flowers to paint, she turned to making pillow lace. Another of her talents was a beautiful soprano voice. But this we did not hear at its best since she overstrained it by singing to my father while carrying all of us. Beyond her family she had few close friends and was chary of showing her feelings. I remember wishing that she would express more affection for our school-friends, similar to that their mothers showed to us. She was not a lover of children, as children, but of her own children because of the deep bond between them. When we hurt ourselves her first reaction was of irritation: "When you hurt yourselves you hurt me." The next was of tenderness. No one could have been more tender and kinder when we were ill. A certain three pound tin of biscuits, all to oneself, was never forgotten at the outset of an illness. I have never seen them since my childhood. I wonder if Huntley & Palmer still make them; they were like tiny, toasted sponge-fingers.

Sundays were, on the whole, very happy days. The snag was the Church Service. The Vicar was very elderly and preached long, dreary sermons. He gave out to his favourite parishioners, not my parents as my father never went to hear him—that he would retire as soon as he felt that his useful work for the church had ended. But that point was never reached. So my mother took us to a livelier church. After lunch she told us exciting Bible stories. Then my father took the three of us out for the afternoon. Sometimes just for a long walk in Kensington Gardens and sometimes to call on friends. And then we stayed to tea. A grown-up and three children. Rather an imposition, one might think. But in those more spacious days we were taken for granted. Possibly, too, the presence of our father outbalanced that of his children. But though we liked going out to tea with our special Sunday friends, the best treat of all was going to the Zoological Gardens. They were only open on Sundays to Fellows of the Society and those to whom they gave Fellows' Tickets. Two of our uncles were Fellows so we went fairly often and, as the Gardens were never crowded, we got to know several of the keepers. Our favourite animals were the Malay Bears, whom we claimed as our own pets, and the inmates of the Little Mammal House. Best of all was the kinkajou which the keeper used to put into my arms. It was so soft and cuddly that I wanted one for my own. But the keeper dissuaded me because it slept all day and was awake all night. Then we had tea. But first my father had to declare that we were bona-fide travellers. That is to say, that we had come more than two miles. In our case this was a fact. If we had come less than two miles we should not have been allowed to buy refreshment on a Sunday. On the way home my father told us fairy tales. Thrilling stories of giants and fairies, of enchanted forests and castles, an endless flow. There was much to think about as we got into the smelly, smoky train that took us from Portland Road to Bishop's Road Station. Sometimes before going into the station we would stand a moment or two in the middle of the road to watch the puffs of black smoke rising from the vent holes let into the road.

One day after a visit to the Zoological Gardens we got home just before dusk. In the shadow of the porch a man was standing. My father paused before putting in his latch-key and looked at the man in the shadow. "Don't you know me, Stebbing?" he said, "I'm Austen." My father put out both his hands. "Come in," he said. The man was Charles Austen, Nigel's godfather and a Correspondent of *The Times* He stayed to dinner and for this very special occasion, we all three were allowed to listen while Mr. Austen talked. He had been in Paris all through its siege by the Germans at the end of the Franco-Prussian War in 1870. He told us of near starvation when leather boots were chopped up and stewed, when rats and mice were killed for food. One dish was "Chat garni des Souris." The chat was quite good eating, but not the souris. Rats, on the other hand, that had lived and fed in the granaries, were much prized. His talk was better than any story-book. Strange to say the only other time that I remember anything of Charles Austen was many years later when a nurse, who was nursing my mother in her last illness, told me that she had nursed Mr. Austen in Oxford shortly before his death. Nigel had been sent a magnificent tricycle horse as a christening present and for years when asked his name said it was "Nigel Austen Stebbing Kia" as the horse had been addressed to "Nigel Austen Stebbing Esquire." I think that the coming of Charles Austen must have awakened in us an interest in history, as I remember one of us asking my father what would happen if we went to war with another country. "We should win," said my father, "but at the end we should be a third-rate Power."

I think we children saw a good deal more of our parents than did most of our contemporaries. For instance, when my mother hired a victoria once a week so as to get through as long a list of "calls" as possible during the summer season, she took Irene and me with her. I doubt if other small girls accompanied their mothers on these formal occasions. We took it in turns to sit facing the horse on the comfortable seat next to my mother, or on the little back seat which, as it could be pushed up out of the way, had no sides to it and you had to hold on tight going round corners. We also took it in turns to ring the door-bell, ask the parlourmaid or man-servant if the lady were at home and hand in the visiting-cards if she were out, or not at home. My mother never took in more than one of us. We always hoped that tea would be ready by the time we called and that it was an "At Home" day, in which case there would be a good tea. These "calls", in spite of our somewhat irregular presence at them, were subject to strict codes of behaviour.

While Irene, Nigel and I were enjoying a very pleasant, if not a very energetic life at home, Will, now at Marlborough under Dr. Bell, a college friend of my father, and Mark, were having a very uncomfort-able time. The preparatory school in Hertfordshire where Will had been and Mark now was, had been highly recommended by friends of my parents. It may have gone down in the intervening years. When our boys were there they were half-starved, neither boy ever touched Jerusalem artichokes in any form for the rest of his life because they said it was the only vegetable they were given, and very little of anything else. Of course none of the details the boys told us ever reached our parents' ears while they were at the school. I am sure my mother would have been shocked to hear that they were scrubbed on their one bath-night a week by an ancient man-servant and his wife.

Marlborough was much nicer than the prep school, but it was dread-fully cold. What good could come from lessons early in the morning when the boys were too cold and hungry to take them in. I do not remember whether the boys had half-term holidays. They certainly never came home during the term, though my parents went to see them. Once, when Nigel had followed Mark to Rugby, my mother took Irene and me to see him there. My chief memory of that visit is the enormous breakfast Nigel and the two friends he brought with him, ate. The landlady at the inn said she knew what boys liked. They began with chops, then went on to sausages and eggs and bacon, finishing with toast and marmalade. At the end they returned to school looking none the worse for their enormous meal. Irene and I, on the other hand, had lovely half-term holidays. We spent them at Headley (our house in the country) and each took a friend down to spend them with us. Irene always took Evelyn Du Pontet whose brother, Clement, she afterwards married.

Miss Carter had left us because we learnt so little from her. This was, probably, due more to our stupidity than to her incompetence. I am driven to this conclusion because the John Macmillans, to whom she

33

went after she left us, spoke of her as so excellent a governess that they wondered why we ever parted with her. I fear the reason is not far to seek. As well as Miss Carter we had a French governess who came two or three times a week. She had married, soon after she came to England, one of the students she was coaching in French. She had been invited to an evening party by Mr. and Mrs. Frederic Harrison whose sons she was teaching. She asked these young men how she should say Good-bye to her hostess in a polite manner. The time arrived. She dropped a little curtsey and said, "It is now time that I take my 'ook". Miss Carter and Madame Princep spent much time discussing their domestic problems. Partly in French, partly in English, to all of which we three listened with all our ears. As we appeared to be absorbed in our own affairs neither governess worried about us. As Madame said to Miss Carter, "These children are too stoopide to take anything in." I remember well the evening when a change of teaching methods was decided upon. My father asked me a question about Queen Anne. I didn't know the answer and burst into tears. Soon after this Irene and I went to Notting Hill High School for the Entrance Examination. It was rather frightening as we had never been set questions to write answers to, before. The sums were easy but I had learnt no grammar. Miss Jones, the Head Mistress, a friend of my parents, stood by me: "The parts of speech?" she began, but met a look of utter blankness. History was better. I wrote a long piece on Joan of Arc, having lately read a story-book about her. The French questions, though we had had a French governess for years, might have been written in Greek. So we were both put in the first form. After the first few days of miserable shyness, I got on fairly well and made many friends. My only criticism of the High School system is that there is too much homework, particularly written work. Many of my friends sat up till ten o'clock doing it. In my case I finished the written work at about eight o'clock and left the memory work till I got to school next morning. A dangerous method if exams are to be passed. I studied a various collection of subjects, including Latin and Greek. I got my father to allow me to change German for Greek, as I disliked the German mistress. For this I am eternally grateful to him. The idea that Latin and Greek are dead languages seems to me absurd, when one considers how many of our words have their roots in them. But it was equally absurd in my day, and even in my sons' day, to spend so large a proportion of time, in both preparatory and public schools, in driving Latin grammar into the heads of boys who would have been far better employed in studying mathematics or science.

34

My mother, though a Londoner and unused to animals, was anxious that we should learn to care for them and look after them. I remember our excitement when my mother, after a week-end visit to the country, put a box on the dining-room table and told us to uncover it. To our joy, inside were two guinea-pigs. They were the first of a succession of guinea-pigs, enough for all of us. They were kept on top of a service-lift which in our day was unused. It was at the end of the passage, just opposite to the kitchen stairs. When they heard the sounds of preparations for dinner and smelt the savoury smells of cooking, they set up a persistent squeaking, which we children, in bed on the second floor, listened for every night before settling off to sleep. We always took them with us on our six weeks summer holiday and made a big run for them on the lawn. But even this change was not enough to keep them in good condition and gradually their numbers declined, until only two were left; a ginger-coloured one belonging to Mark and my Ruby, white with pink eyes. One day only Ruby was left. She looked poorly but my mother revived her with a few spoonfuls of milk with drops of brandy in it. She seemed quite herself again. But one Sunday when we got home from church she was dead. "If only," I cried, "we had not gone to church, Mother would have given her brandy and she would be still alive."

My mother used to tell us about a squirrel which lived in a small house in Notting Hill which they shared with my grandfather for the first year or so after marriage. It was called Skug as it came from Berkshire, skug being the Berkshire name for a squirrel. Skug had the run of the house and always shared their breakfast. One day he got onto the table before they were down and ate a whole butterball and was very sick. He used to bury some of his nuts in the window-box outside the dining-room window, following his instinct to provide for the winter. A few years after they had left the house my mother called on friends who had taken the house and was amused to see a nice little hazelnut tree outside the dining-room window. Before Will was born my parents moved to Russell Square and after that the rest of us arrived in such quick succession that other pets were out of the question. But not long after the last of the guinea-pigs had died my mother took me with her to buy a squirrel. The pet-shop we went to was in Seven Dials. A narrow, dingy little street leading from Tottenham Court Road towards Charing Cross, and now swept away. There were thin, ragged children playing in the street and my mother held her hand over her pocket, close to the plaquet of her skirt. To me their rags were repulsive and I clung the closer to my mother's arm. Though both my parents were generous to those whose needs they understood, I never saw them give to beggars. It was as if their state of existence was beyond their comprehension. The shop we were looking for had some puppies and kittens in the dirty window. A man stood in the dark entrance. My mother asked if he had any young squirrels. He said some had just arrived. We bought one, it was put into a brown paper bag and I, feeling very important, carried it home.

We, of course, took Skug with us for our holidays. One year we spent a few weeks on Rose Hill in Dorking. Just beyond the garden was a wood. Not a safe place for a tame squirrel unused to cats and wild squirrels, so we kept Skug indoors. One day I left the garden door open. Skug was through it, across the lawn and into the wood in a flash. I was abused and knew I deserved every word of it. Not one of the other children spoke to me that afternoon. To make matters worse, we returned to London that day. My mother took Skug's cage to friends who were staying in the next door house and asked if they would put it, for the night, by an open window overlooking the garden. This they agreed to do. Next morning a telegram arrived for my mother. "Skug safely back in cage". She took the next train back to Dorking and brought Skug home. She found him fast asleep in a cage full of empty nutshells, as though he had neither eaten nor slept since he left home the day before. The wild squirrels had probably nearly scared him to death. This, or another of our Skugs, had another adventure, one quite unique in the lives of squirrels. A night spent in *The Times* office, Printing House Square. When my father arrived at the office one night, he hung up his coat and happened to put his hand into a pocket. In it was something warm and soft. It was Skug, fast asleep. Not knowing what else to do, he left him there. And there he was, still asleep, next morning.

There is much talk in these days of the folly of "keeping up with the Joneses": rather as if it were something modern. In my young days we were just as silly. To prove that one belonged to the fashionable world the whole family must leave London as soon as the Season was over. That is to say as soon as that important social function, Goodwood Races, was over. After that, though, you might go out for a walk without a coat over your summer frock and silk or cotton gloves might replace those of kid or suede. Yet the sooner you and yours left London to the hordes of those who never left it, the better for your place in Society. Curtains were taken down, all the furniture was covered in dust sheets. No one entered or left by the front door. It was whispered that, when some member of the family had, for business or other reasons, to remain in London, he slunk in and out of the house by the area steps. Another case of a good position in Society being fixed for you, was the dinner hour. When this was raised from 7.30 to 8 o'clock friends of mine told me that some connections of theirs living in a fashionable quarter of the town, instructed their coachman to pick them up round the corner, for fear lest the footmen standing about the doors should notice that they were dining with lesser folk who still dined at an unfashionable hour.

There were strict rules of conduct about "calls". For instance, if a lady—the term woman was not used in my youth—had her own carriage she might send it out with a footman or even a page boy on the box, and he might deliver his mistress's cards. When handing him the cards she would instruct him as to whether she would or would not enter the house should the lady be at home. If she did not intend to leave her carriage she would turn down a corner of a card to indicate that she had actually been at the door. Merely to send cards round by a servant was looked on with much disfavour by the ladies who thus received them. Most ladies had their "At Home" day printed on their cards, and it was correct to call on this day. But with so many calls to make in the Season this was not always possible especially as some ladies chose the first and third Monday, or some such day, that was impossible to remember. My mother's day was Tuesday. By 3 o'clock the parlour-maid and housemaid were dressed in their black afternoon dresses with dainty muslin caps. Not a bit like those ugly creations with flaps hanging down behind, that Stage domestics wear. A well-dressed parlourmaid was as essential to the look of the house as its curtains and its front door brass knobs. The best china tea-service was laid out in the drawing-room. The tea was the most expensive blended China and Indian tea. There was the thinnest brown and white bread and butter, sandwiches and little cakes. After an "At Home" or "Evening Party" there might be many callers. Irene and I dressed in Sunday frocks with muslin pinafores, and Nigel in a sailor suit, came into the drawing-room after our schoolroom tea and played in the bay window among the aspidistras and ferns. We used to talk as we thought the grown-ups talked, mimicking secretly their gestures and movements. After a while Nigel refused to join Irene and me, in spite of the lure of cakes. He said "they would kiss him."

An outing we all enjoyed very much was Show Sunday, just before the opening day of the Royal Academy Summer Exhibition. We would start in a friend's studio, look at his pictures, have tea and go on to other studios to which we had been given introductions. It was great fun. As well as meeting many interesting artists and their families we used to count up how many teas we had eaten. The Briton Rivieres were great friends of ours. The artists I remember best, after them, were the Alfred Hunts and his charming water-colours of Whitby: and Mr. Marshall who painted London scenes. The Holman Hunts we saw a good deal of while I was growing up. They were one of the Sunday friends my father used to take us to visit. Some of his paintings we watched as they progressed from stage to stage. If he were painting a figure he would paint it first in the nude and then clothe it. This was so, if my memory does not fail me, in "the Lady of Shalott". I remember, too the incomplete painting of his daughter Gladys at the age of fifteen. He should, he told us, have painted her before sitting to him had become so tiresome. There was, indeed, a look of boredom on her handsome face. The Alfred Hunts, too, were special Sunday friends. I was disappointed when I found on our first visit to them, that the youngest daughter, Sylvia, was not a little girl like me.

Some of my happiest memories are of garden parties. Hay-making parties in Sir Spencer and Lady Wells' lovely grounds to which our whole family was invited and which we went up to for several years after we left Hampstead. There was a lake which we looked at with longing eyes but it was reserved for the son of the house and his chosen guests. My last memory of Sir Spencer is of a very old gentle-faced man in an armchair with one Siamese kitten on one shoulder and two kittens on the other. Another splendid garden party was given year after year by Mrs. Winkworth at Holly Lodge on Campden Hill. Here, too, the whole family was invited. Here we always met the Sorabji sisters. One of them told my father that God always sent Mrs. Winkworth a fine day for her party. And, indeed, I do not remember a wet one. There was a never-ending supply of strawberries and cream. A story one of the Sorabji sisters told us pleased us very much. She, and her two little sisters, were out in the forest near their home, with their French governess. Suddenly appeared in front of them a great wild beast. The governess turned and fled. The three little girls, remembering what they had been told, held hands and stared at the animal which lowered its eyes and slunk off. When the children returned to their palace the governess had already been sent away.

Among the guests we always met at Holly Lodge was Sir Lewis Morris. Unlike some of the grown-ups of our acquaintance, he never failed to remember and greet Irene and me. He was not a very popular member of our Society. Rumour had it that he was not, in fact, the bachelor he posed as being, but that he had a wife and children in

London. This was very disturbing as one or two matrons had busied themselves in finding a suitable partner for him. It was Dr. Rutherford, Headmaster of Westminster, where Sir Lewis's son was a pupil, who brought the story to light. It was very unfair on the family, he insisted. Sir Lewis's excuse was that his means were not sufficient to keep them all in Society.

About this time Tennyson died and left the post of Poet Laureate vacant. Dr. Rutherford told my father that Sir Lewis had said to him, "There seems to be a conspiracy of silence about my claims to be Poet Laureate. What would you advise me to do about it?" "Join it," said Dr. Rutherford. Soon after this Sir Lewis brought his wife and daughter to call on my mother. I remember them well. Both were tall and goodlooking. Lady Morris spoke in a low, husky voice as though she had not quite recovered from an attack of laryngitis.

Another pleasant garden party was at Miss Jean Ingelow's house in Kensington. She lived with her architect brother in a small terrace of houses each of which had a small garden entered through French windows from the drawing-room. Miss Ingelow's great friend was the singer, Antoinette Sterling. They were an odd pair. The poet, small, timid, with a sweet smile but not a word to say for herself. The singer, tall, imposing, with bold black eyes and a ready tongue. Her husband, Mr. McKinlay, always looked as if he wondered whatever his wife was going to say next, but whatever it was he refused to be embarrassed. At this house, too, children were welcome guests; we enjoyed the ices and strawberries. When Jean Ingelow died some of the guests at her graveside were scandalized by Antoinette Sterling bursting into song. It was, I think, a very touching tribute of affection.

4   Bicycles, Pets and Adventures Abroad

M^y grandfather left his house at Little Warley to my mother, but it
was a long journey to Liverpool Street station from our London
house, so my parents made up their minds to sell Warley Elms and
buy a cottage in Surrey. Before selling the house we all spent a couple
of summer months in it. There was a huge cedar tree on the lawn in
front of the house. Under its spreading branches we made our house.
At first we were content to scrounge what food we could from the
cook and pretend to cook in in an old saucepan we found on the kitchen
midden. We collected a few bricks and made a fireplace. But it would
be more fun to make a real fire, boil the saucepan of water over it and
make our own tea and even stew our own fruit. I was to be cook and
already had many schemes. The boys got matches from the drawing-
room and lighted the pine needles. They caught at once and I put the
saucepan on top. We had got some flour and milk from the cook, who
gave them to get rid of us. I was planning how to get round her for
other ingredients when Gregory, the old man-servant, burst in and
put out our lovely fire. He said that soon the whole tree would have
been burnt to the ground. He was a good sport and promised that he
would not tell on us if we promised never to light a fire again. Gregory
had been with my grandfather for many years and he stayed with us
until the house was sold. Then with the legacy my grandfather had
left him, he bought a small inn in the neighbourhood, married the
kitchen-maid— to the disgust of the superior maids—and set up as
an inn-keeper. Their first child was called after me.

As soon as Warley Elms was sold my parents began to look for a
cottage on the South-Eastern or Southern lines. One snowy winter's
day they set off to look at a house the Agent thought might suit them.
"Go," he said, "to Betchworth Station and there you can get a fly to
take you to the house. It is only two miles away." The fly was old

and stuffy, the driver said it would be 'ard on the 'orse in such weather. At the foot of a steep-looking hill the driver said they must get out and walk. My parents looked at one another. "Take us back to the station," they said. They didn't fancy a house at the top of such a hill. Soon afterwards another Agent sent the description of a house, near, he said, to Leatherhead. It was a pleasant five mile drive along winding country lanes and the house was on the very edge of a common. "Lovely for the children," said my mother. That evening my father sent an offer for the house. It was not as large as the owners hoped for, but it had been for sale for a long time and the owners were anxious to leave. So the offer was accepted. Of course we were eager for every detail, but all they told us was to wait and see it. A few days later my mother went into the library laughing. "Look", she said, "the house we went to see from Betchworth and the house we saw from Leatherhead, are the very same house." She showed the Agents' descriptions of the house.

It was the beginning of the Easter holidays that my mother, the five of us, and four maids, began the drive from Leatherhead to Headley. At every turning we shouted "Are we near?" Every house we saw we asked, "Is it that?" When we came to one gate and then a second across a road through a farm, we all wanted to get down and open and shut the gates. This was really country.

When we reached the house we tumbled out of the fly as one man. The front door was open and a smiling middle-aged woman stood on the doorstep. We shouted, "It isn't a cottage, it's quite a big house." My mother looked rather annoyed. She did not like noisy demonstrations, particularly in front of a domestic. This woman, with her fifteen year old son, was to look after the house when we were not there and help our maids when we were living there. The boy was to clean the boots and shoes, but his chief task was to pump up the water from the well, as there was no water laid on. The house was built on a slope so that the drawing-room was raised above the garden and had a glorious view of the Mickleham Downs, while the kitchen beneath the drawing-room also had a view of the garden. There was a pond in front of the house and the boys soon made a raft to sail on it. I remember our anger, one Christmas holiday, to find that some people we knew, who lived in a big house not far off, had sent their ice-cart to strip all the ice off our pond to put into their ice-pit for use in the summer.

There was a good garden with a tennis court at the garden front of the house, and a cottage and a bit of common before you came to the kitchen gardens, the gardener's cottage and the stables. Almost best of all was the common. This was our playground. We never met anyone else there. We explored every foot of it. There were two valleys—one I called the Valley of Bones, because there were so many skulls and other rabbit bones there. There were forests of blackberry bushes and wild roses with honeysuckle climbing over them. And there were trees to climb and hundreds of paths covered with springy turf. In the autumn there was heather, and bracken so tall you were hidden in it. Mr. Chamberlain, our Rector, told us that once after he had been dining with the Dudley Ryders at High Ashurst, he had lost his way going home across the Common and had had to stay in the bracken till it was light enough to see his way out. We got to know all the people in the village and loved them. We played cricket matches with the choirboys, but could not get the girls to join Irene and me. Our gardener, Dunmall, was a great character. He told us he knew the number of every hymn in the hymnbook, and though we often tried to catch him out, we never succeeded. His children, Freddie and Jessie, were about two and three when we went to Heath House. A third child arrived soon after, and Dunmall wanted her to be called Ivorine. When my mother said that meant sham ivory the name was changed to Yvonne. Dunmall used to take us to find birds' nests—not so as to collect eggs but to show us the different sorts. One day he came up to us with the back of a hand against his mouth. "Come out after you've had your supper," he whispered, "I'll have something to show you." We met him when it was beginning to get dark. He did not speak but led us up and down a path on to the Common. Here he motioned to us not to speak and pointed. There lay a dead fox. Dunmall jerked its brush and Mark jumped back a pace or two. "Don't say anything to anybody," he said, "but someone lost so many of his chickens that he came out and shot the brute." We knew the feeling about foxes in the village and wouldn't have split for anything.

One of our friends in Betchworth gave us a ginger-coloured kitten. We called it Marmalade. One holiday we could not find her anywhere. We were much distressed and looked for her everywhere. One morning our parents told us that the previous evening while they were walking in the kitchen-garden Marmalade had jumped in front of them out of a rhubarb-bed. We rushed out but no Marmalade was to be seen. But a cosy little nest had been made. "She must have had kittens," my mother said, "and she did not want you to see them yet." A week or two later I dropped a ball out of the schoolroom window into some bushes. I jumped out and felt under them; something soft and furry bit and scratched my hand. I shouted for the others to help me. "Put on gloves," I said. Together we pulled out four fluffy little demons. Clever Marmalade had moved her kittens near enough to the house for her to get milk and food, but still well-hidden from us. We took them into a shed near the house and gradually they became tame. When Marmalade got bored with them we found them good homes. Another pet was a baby rabbit which Dunmall had chased and caught. It became very tame and followed us everywhere. When we went back to school my parents stayed at Headley a day or two longer. After we had gone they took our rabbit on to the common after dinner. Next morning the rabbit was waiting for them in the kitchen garden. They picked it up and kept it with them till evening. Again they took it on to the common. And that was the last they saw of it. I have another memory about rabbits. As it was sometimes difficult to get any meat but pork at Headley, my mother bought some young rabbits from someone who bred them. She gave them to Jackson, who looked after the stables, to feed. They were white and very pretty. We each adopted one of them and tied different coloured ribbons round their necks so as to know them apart. One day there was stewed rabbit for lunch. "No thank you," said Irene and I, and Will and Nigel, as the parlourmaid took the plates round. Only Mark, always the hungriest of us, took the plate offered to him. The rabbits bought for food we had turned into pets and we would not eat them. Perhaps the maids ate the rest. They were not served up to us.

When I was about thirteen Uncle George Pinckard gave me an Exmoor pony and he added much to our enjoyment of all our holidays. Both Irene and I rode him and learnt his tricks. He was always impatient to start so the moment one foot was in a stirrup he was off, and one mounted as best one could. Of course in those days we rode side-saddle. Even small girls would have been looked on as hoydens if they had ridden astride. Puck would not pass a piece of paper blowing about in the road, or a tramp sitting by the roadside. One had to dismount and lead him past. Once when a rainstorm had flooded part of a road and Puck was harnessed to the pony-cart, he lay down and would not move till the coachman got down and led him through the water. One day I saw an old woman sitting on the ground, smoking a clay-pipe. By her side lay a long canvas bag. Puck of course would not pass her. I jumped down and began to lead him past. The old woman picked up the bag, untied it and pulled out a long, white cat. After a few minutes she put the cat back in the bag, tied it up, slung the bag over her shoulder and made off down the hill. When we grew too big to ride him we sold him to friends with a young family. When they came to visit us, Puck trotted faster and faster as he neared his old stable.

I remembered well two rides over Epsom Downs. One was just before the Spring Meeting. The Downs were full of gypsy caravans and tents. Brown-faced children were running about and there was a good smell rising from the chimneys. I thought of what our doctor, Dr. Daniel, had told us. He was a good friend to the gypsies, attending them for nothing and listening to their troubles. One day he said to a group of them, "I hear many complaints from people of losing chickens while you are up here." "You won't lose any chickens, Doctor," they assured him. A few days later I again crossed the Downs. The whole ground was smothered with scraps of dirty paper and other rubbish. It must have taken days to clear it up. I never met any unpleasantness while I was riding, but we heard that some ladies who had been foolish enough to ride, attended by a groom, on Box Hill on an August Bank Holiday, had been shouted at and the groom pulled from his horse. The blame lay with people who had not the good sense to respect the Londoners' playground.

Cherkley Court was the scene of several amusing incidents while we lived at Headley. My father sometimes took Irene and me over there to tea with Mr. and Mrs. Dixon on a Sunday. Mr. Dixon's delight was in his greenhouse. There was a range of them, three or four I think, each one hotter than the one before, the last was hot enough to grow ripe bananas—though they were not good to eat—and waterlilies with leaves strong enough to support a small child. At the entrance to these houses Mr. Dixon had placed on either side one of those mirrors that make you look either very fat and short or very thin and tall. A little boy, seeing himself in one of them, was so alarmed that he rushed straight through the glass door leading into the first conservatory. The boy was unhurt. My father, who loved children, said it served Mr. Dixon right for putting such monstrosities in his house. The house was a huge Victorian stuccoed mansion, with a flight of stone steps, with pillars and canopy, leading to the front door. It was once burnt down and Mr. Dixon had it built up again exactly as it was before. After his death the two unmarried daughters gave a dance for their young friends. The great rooms were a splendid setting for a dance. The band was good, so was the supper. We were all set for a night of enjoyment. Suddenly a door was flung open at the top of the main staircase and the figure of Mrs. Dixon in a voluminous white dressing-gown appeared. "What is this noise? Stop it at once," it said. "God save the Queen," was played and we all slunk silently home. Another country dance also ended abruptly. This time it was at an old house at Leatherhead with a garden leading down to the Mole. As the clock in the centre of the town began to strike the hour of midnight, the National Anthem again cut us off in the middle of a dance. It was our host's bedtime.

My mother wanted a man who could look after chickens as well as after the pony. There was plenty of room for a man and wife over the stables. One evening she took me with her to interview a man who was leaving a post as odd-job man at Cherkley Court. He had quite a good character but he and his wife had a small son and Mr. Dixon did not like boys. A nice tidy woman opened the cottage door and told us her husband had just got in from work and would see us in a minute or two. Then followed a great splashing of water. When that ceased, Mrs. Jackson returned, closely followed by her husband. She nudged him and he pulled a lock of damp hair. Another nudge and he said, "Evening Ma'am". My mother asked him a few questions; he answered prompted by his wife. Mrs. Jackson assured my mother that her husband was honest and respectable and he was engaged. They lived with us for many years and were a delightful couple. When we left Heath House they moved with us to Frith Park and lived in the farm-house. When we returned to town after the holidays Jackson used to drive up the seventeen miles once a week bringing vegetables and fruit and eggs and chickens in a little van. He told us that he always tried to drive through the gates into the Park at Hyde Park Corner, but the Park Keeper always stopped him and said that way was only for private carriages. "Ain't this a private carriage? I asks him— Look, it's got Mr. Stebbing's name and address on it. But he won't let me through."

It was shortly after we went to Headley that one of the greatest excitements of my early teens came about. We all learnt to bicycle. My first lessons were on Mark's bicycle. So as not to injure myself by inevitable falls from his 'safety bicycle', so called to distinguish it from its predecessor, the 'penny-farthing bicycle', I learnt on the grass of Headley cricket-field: probably very near the pitch as the process of eradicating the gorse was slow. When we returned to London after the summer holidays Irene and I had lessons at Queen's Club. After that, we, and a great concourse of more or less fashionable young people paraded up and down the road inside Hyde Park, girls and young men alike, on Saturday mornings throughout one spring and summer. The girls all wore ankle-length skirts with two bit of elastic sewn to the hem, to be fastened round the ankles, so as to prevent the skirt from blowing up and exposing an unbecoming amount of female leg. I remember the first time I saw a young woman on a bicycle in bloomers. It was in Kensington High Street. As she passed a butcher's boy on a bicycle he dismounted and called after her, "You naughty girl." In my early cycling days I had a slight accident. Nigel and I were cycling along Gloucester Terrace. A hansom drove along from Paddington station towards Craven Hill. As it crossed Gloucester Terrace Nigel turned to avoid it but I went straight on, slap into the wheels. I was unhurt but the front mudguard of my bicycle was buckled.

The era of the bicycle marked the beginning of the emancipation of girls in the middle class. Very few of their mothers learnt to ride. Those who did learn were chiefly spinsters and middle-aged widows. My aunt, Beatrice Batty, bought a low-geared machine and rode it all over Oxford. But she was looked on as eccentric. As for the mothers of bicycling daughters they must have felt rather like hens that have brought up a brood of ducklings and seen them taking to the water. I do not remember my mother making any complaint when Irene and I bought bicycles out of our own savings—probably from the ten shillings a month allowance for ribbons and gloves. And when the bicycles were bought, and kept in the schoolroom, nor did she try to stop our rides with girl friends as far afield as Battersea Park. Perhaps older women, even the more old-fashioned married women, sensed that the time was coming when their closely-guarded daughters would break out of the nets drawn around them by the husbands and fathers. And then the wiser of them would aid and abet them.

In the spring of 1886 our parents took Irene and me to Italy for six weeks. We had often complained that they had given up going abroad just at the time when we could have gone with them. Now they had listened to our complaint and on February 12th we left London by the night train, arriving in Paris about 5 a.m. Bedrooms had been booked for us but Irene and I were far too excited to sleep. Leaving my mother in bed my father, Irene and I started out about nine o'clock to see Paris, for my father was as anxious to show us the sights of Paris as we were to see them. The boulevards, the Seine and the bridges, the churches, the shops, we saw them all. We had dinner at our hotel before leaving by the night express for Pisa. One course of that dinner I remember. It was sole with mussel sauce. I did not like the idea of eating mussels but my mother said they were delicious. Although we travelled first class the night seemed very long and we were all awake

46

before daybreak. I remember that early morning because my mother looked rather unhappy. Then my father put a little envelope into her hand and she was all smiles. The date was Valentine's Day and my father had not forgotten to buy a handpainted card before we left London and to write verses on it, "To my Valentine" as he had done every year since their marriage in 1870. We had left London two days before with its pale and shadowy light and here in Pisa we were dazzled by the sunlight on white houses, white streets and pavements. Even the trees, still leafless, seemed to have white trunks. There seemed no shady side of the streets. We were quite glad to return to the train, and be on our way to Rome. We stayed in Marini's Hotel, at the end of Via Tritoni, close to the Houses of Parliament. It was a medium-sized, comfortable hotel, well-known to my parents. The proprietor's wife was English. My mother was down to breakfast the first morning before my father. There was some delay in bringing our coffee and rolls—caused, the waiter said, by their being so upset by an old gentleman falling on the polished marble floor in the hall. The old gentleman was my father. An American doctor staying in the hotel had bound up a deep cut in his head, but the proprietor had sent for an Italian doctor. This doctor looked at the bandage, said it looked all right, and sent in a large bill. Until the bandage could be discarded, my father would not leave the hotel. Fortunately for Irene and me, a friend of his, a retired Foreign Correspondent of *The Times*, Mr. Stillman, lived with his wife and two beautiful daughters, Liza and Effie, in Rome. Both girls were six foot tall—next to them Irene and I must have looked like insignificant dwarfs. They devoted themselves to us and took us all over the city. One day they took us for a lunch-picnic in the Campagna. We drove there in an open carriage with a coachman and a footman. Without these two men it would not have been safe to venture so far from the city, for fear of brigands.

As soon as my father was able to leave the hotel we explored Rome, far more thoroughly than we had done with Liza and Effie—too thoroughly for our taste. We went into every church, for fear we might miss some priceless fresco or painting in its dim interior. One day as we were returning to the hotel for lunch, we had to make our way through a crowd of people massed in front of the Houses of Parliament. They were shouting "Death to Crispi! Down with Crispi!" Crispi was Prime Minister. News of a great Italian defeat by the Ethiopians had just reached Rome. That night my father, Irene and I, went for a walk after dinner. The streets were almost deserted and totally quiet. We walked up to the Capitol. On every step crouched a soldier, rifle at the ready. The Government were fearful of the populace in their present mood. Next morning placards all over the city announced that a solemn Te Deum would be sung in St. Peter's. We went into St. Peter's soon afterwards. It was draped in hangings of black and purple, a strange and moving sight. Next day we left Rome for Florence. Of Florence, though of all the cities on the Continent known to me, I loved most, I have no particular memories. Of Venice I have a few, two of them still vivid. The first is being in a gondola on the Grand Canal. A lovely quiet night—broken suddenly by gondoliers singing. And the song they sang was Ta-ra-ta Boomdeay! The second memory is of standing on the Bridge of Sighs. We heard shouts and saw a number of people running towards us. Then a gondola passed rapidly under the bridge. In it a man sat huddled, his face buried in his arms. We made out what the crowd were saying. "He has murdered someone," then, "He has murdered his mother." The gondola passed under the Bridge of Sighs to the prison beyond. There was no capital punishment in Italy, so we knew that this man was going to solitary confinement and never again would speak to a living soul beyond his gaoler and, I hope, his priest.

It was very hot in April that year. There was a heatwave all over Europe and we were glad to find some pleasant public gardens not far from the Grand Canal. The evenings we spent in the Cathedral Piazza where we never could decide whether the ices in the cafe on the right of the Piazza were better than the ices on the left of the Piazza, or the other way about. Our last week in Italy was a lovely restful one, at Menaggio on Lake Maggiore. Here there were no monuments to look at. Only beautiful walks along the lake and trips on the little steamers. The last night of our tour was spent in Paris. It was Easter week and Paris was so crowed that our hotel could only let us have two single rooms. Not a very comfortable night for any of us. But the evening had one remarkable feature, though I doubt if any of the four of us was capable of judging its significance. The hotel proprietor asked if we would care to listen from his sittingroom, to the music of the opera being performed at that moment at the Opera House. It was a travesty of the music, no doubt, but there it was. Live music direct from the Opera House to our ears in that Paris sitting-room. When some time later I thought of that wireless music relayed to us in 1896 from the Paris Opera House, I was reminded of a remark made by my father years earlier. He told us that his future brother-in-law, Robert Braithwaite Batty, Third Wrangler of his year at Cambridge, told him that some day we should be able to hear sounds transmitted by waves through the air. At present, he said, we have not learnt how to do it. As my uncle Robert was at the time coaching my father in mathematics, some slight knowledge of this subject being necessary for entrance into Oxford, the year must have been about 1850.

Next day we were home again.

Before going to Italy my parents had sold Heath House and bought a much a larger house in the next village, Walton-on-the-Hill. It was called Frith Park. It had beautiful grounds, park-land and woods and a garden big enough for three tennis courts. The gardens had been laid out by a landscape gardener and there was a charming little five-acre wood leading out of the gardens, blue with hyacinths in the spring. There was another wood with an acre of wild lilies-of-the-valley. But these were dug up by vandals until none were left.

Another rather rare plant grew in our lane. Close to a footpath leading into Queen's Wood, there was a Martagan Lily. And where there was a clearing a forest of foxgloves sprang up but one could wander for hours without touching a road or meeting a soul. Yet I missed the friendliness of the smaller village. My mother, too, though she always fell in with my father's wishes, must have found the larger house, as well as the flat in town, a considerable burden, even though we had now a much-loved housekeeper, Miss Martin.

We missed our Headley friends, the men and women, the boys and girls, whom we knew and liked so much. At Walton the people were not nearly so friendly. This was partly due to the rector, who let it be known, for reasons best known to himself, that he did not wish people to interfere with his villagers. Of course the village was a great deal bigger, and so we did not have the same opportunity of getting to know the villagers.

There were far more guests than had been possible at Heath House, and tennis parties. These were a delight to my father, but an extra source of anxiety for my mother; there were very few shops in Walton village and much had to be ordered from London. At Headley where there were only two shops, a baker's and the general shop cum Post Office, Mr. Braithwaite, the Postmaster, shopped for us in Leatherhead on Saturdays. Sometimes, as he was a keen cricketer, he could not spare the time from a match to drive down to Leatherhead. So, in the hottest part of the year, we ate nothing but pork, which Mr. Braithwaite himself provided. At Headley, too, we all walked the twenty minutes walk to church, including, to our surprise, our father who never went to church in London. At Walton we usually drove to church. The rector was a hunting man and was rather scornful of his office saying that he had only gone into the Church because his father owned the living and told him it was that or nothing. He treated his own son, who wished to be an actor, in the same way. The son, however, turned out to be a very tolerable parson, without his father's desire to keep the parish as his private preserve.

5   *Growing Up*

My last year or two at school saw the beginning of a period of great
upheavals in the life of women. Many were becoming dissatisfied
with the role allotted to them by men. They wanted more say in the running of their lives. Why, they asked, should they be debarred from enter-
ing the professions? The only two careers open to them, teaching and
nursing, were shockingly badly paid. With the education now open to
them in the High Schools, they were as capable as men of becoming
doctors, yet the doors of all the teaching hospitals were closed to them.
In spite of this a few determined women became fully-qualified doctors.
When both Oxford and Cambridge refused to give degrees to women,
however well they had done in the examinations, some went to lesser
Universities and were granted degrees by them. One of these was
Aberystwyth and all honour to that broad-minded University. Although
the mistresses at the High Schools were well-qualified, their salaries
were still very inadequate. I remember very well the young mistress,
fresh from Oxford, who took the First Form when I went into it at
Notting Hill. She took every subject, except French and Scripture
which were taken by Miss Jones, the Head Mistress. This young
mistress's salary was, I was told, £18 a year. What salary a young
graduate at King's College for Ladies in Kensington Square, received,
I do not know. But when she asked me to tea with her in a small
poorly-furnished workman's flat—all I suppose, that she could afford—
I was shocked to find that a girl like myself should be obliged to live in
such conditions.

Soon after our return from Italy I called on very dear friends of my
family, the Misses Mary and Margaret Eve, who seemed to me to
combine an intellectual and gracious way of living, with a deep interest
in those whose lot was not as fortunate as theirs. Margaret was an
active member of the London School Board. Both she and Mary took

much interest in the female teachers in the Board Schools, particularly in the Head Teachers. They did not think that any of them had had enough training for their important tasks. To help in giving them a broader outlook on life they took a different party of six or seven Head Mistresses for a fortnight to Italy, every year; a week in Florence and a week in Venice. In those days good pensions in Florence cost six lire a day for a week's stay, and in Venice seven lire. Railway fares for a party were low, too. Even so, it must have entailed a long period of saving for teachers whose salaries were pitifully low. Yet, year after year, Mary and Margaret Eve took a small party of them to Italy. Telling them what books to borrow from the Lending Libraries, in preparation for the great—probably the only great adventure of their lives. One year I was invited to join them. Our party consisted of five Head Mistresses, one junior teacher whose training seemed to have been more thorough than that of her seniors, myself and the two Miss Eves. Our daily routine had been carefully worked out, so as to give as much instruction as our party was likely to absorb, while making the whole holiday enjoyable. So each morning we studied one of the glorious buildings of Florence or Venice and in the afternoons relaxed.

Two afternoon excursions stand out most vividly in my memory. One to a villa in Fiesole where friends of Mary and Margaret lived. It was a white-stuccoed villa with green shutters, now closely shut to keep out the hot afternoon sun. As Mr. and Mrs. Searle were shepherding our party to a shady part of the orchard, for it was a very hot April day, Mrs. Searle spied a man pulling olives off a tree at the bottom of the sloping orchard. Elderly as she was, she hurried towards him calling to the gardener to assist her. He did not stir, so she tackled the youth, who looked about sixteen, alone. She pulled him to the ground, while he, sobbing loudly, spluttered out that he was hungry and had no money to buy food. Mrs. Searle asked her husband to fetch food, and while the boy ate, she gave him a long lecture. The gardener, who had now strolled up, viewed the scene with a tolerant smile. Another afternoon we visited a young Englishman who had bought an olive plantation outside Florence. A lovely spot with deep-crimson wild tulips in full bloom, under the dark olive trees. Their gnarled branches giving them a look of trees old before their time, like dissipated youths. Our host took us into a shed, full of huge vats filled to the brim with golden oil. He invited us to dip a finger into the oil and taste its freshness. Margaret Eve, being short-sighted, dipped a black-gloved finger in too far and brought it out dripping with oil.

Later on the teachers began to show signs of mental fatigue. They preferred the shops to the monuments. Mary, in particular, seemed a little uneasy when their attention wandered while she was dilating on the carvings on Giotto's Campanile. She was so anxious that they should go home with minds, not only more stored with, but more able to appreciate, beauty.

Not long after our return from Italy, I asked the sisters to show me some of the work they did in the London Schools. Margaret took me to a Meeting of the London School Board in the fine new building of the L.C.C., and Mary took me to some of the Special Schools in which she was greatly interested. One of these was in the Passmore Edwards Settlement, where I saw a class for deaf boys.

But it was the School for Blind Children in Camden Town that aroused all my sympathy, and became, until I was married, one of the main interests of my life. It was a branch of the Brecknock Board School and had in each of its two classes, I think, fifteen or sixteen children, the youngest five years old and the eldest about fourteen. Both the teachers were blind women. Miss Butler had been totally blind from birth: her assistant, Miss Smith, could distinguish between light and dark, but that was all. Both had been trained at the Normal College for the Blind, in London, and were two of the most charming women I have met. Their love for the children and the love of the children for them was delightful to see. When, later on, the School Board decided that the Head Teacher must be sighted, and Miss Butler became Assistant, the school lost some of its charm. It struck me that as blind children, though all learnt to read Braille, had very few children's books to choose from, one of their great needs was to have books read to them. So I went one afternoon a week to the Brecknock School, and another afternoon to a similar school in another part of London, and read to all the children the books that I had liked when I was a child. As the ages varied from five to fourteen the choice of suitable books was a little difficult, but the five and six year olds probably slept and some of the others gave most of their attention to the knitting or other handiwork they were doing at the time. At all events they all greeted me as an old friend and I was much touched when, on bringing them strawberries one day, one of the bigger boys said, "I always thought Miss Stebbing was kind but I never knew before that she was so kind." I have always remembered that these children were the only ones who saw the sun shine on my wedding day. Miss Butler had taken the whole school out into the playground at 2.30 to wish me happiness, "And," said Miss Butler, "at that moment the sun shone.'' I suppose it is just possible that the sun shone at Camden Town, though it certainly did not shine at Walton Heath. At any rate their wish came true.

The other Blind School does not leave so clear an impression on my mind as the Brecknock School. The Head Teacher was sighted and efficient. But the place did not give one the feeling of being lived in by one happy family, as did the other. I remember being amused by one small girl who said to me at the time of a General Election, ''My dad's going to vote for the Conservative, 'cos he says he's such a gentleman.'' My other memory connected with the school is of the journey there, on top of an open-decked, horse-drawn bus. I always travelled on top and as close to the front as I could get. A privileged passenger might even sit on a seat next to the driver. After a while the driver of the bus I always took, at the same time on the same afternoon every week, got to know me and let me sit on the coveted seat. He drove a spanking pair of bays which were used on Sundays by the Territorials and were kept in fine condition, unlike the poor animals that pulled many of the buses. Particularly those on the pirate buses, their life was hard and short. These buses did not belong to a recognised Company, and they tried, by dodging in and out of the traffic, to pick up unwary passengers.

To the child of today, accustomed to freedom from parental control from a very early age, our life would have seemed intolerably restricted. Until we went to school when Nigel was nine and Irene and I were ten and eleven, we had never left the house unaccompanied by a grown-up person. When Nigel refused to walk to school with us, after the first few days, because the other boys would laugh at him, it caused so much astonishment in the household that our cook used to get on a chair, in order to see through the area railings so young a boy going off by himself. As for Irene and me, the schoolroom maid took us to school and was at the school-gate to walk home with us. This continued for years and I do not remember that either of us felt upset by so ridiculous a system, or felt annoyed by it, even though it was a strange proceeding even for those days, and for pupils at a High School. We were certainly never laughed at. Possibly the fact that our parents were friends of Miss Jones, the Head Mistress, and Miss Hannah, her sister, put us in rather a special category. I remember my embarrassment when, meeting me one day in the Big Hall, Miss Jones kissed me. She was an excellent Head Mistress but her views on the education of girls were a little narrow. There came a time when the Board of Governors decreed that needlework should be taught in the school as a compulsory subject. Miss Jones said it was not a suitable subject to be taught in a High School. But the Board was adamant. The only concession agreed to was that the Sixth Form girls should take it or not, as they choose. I was then in the Sixth. Miss Jones informed us of the Board's decision. Not one of the Sixth took sewing. When I went to her sitting-room to say Goodbye on my last day at school Miss Jones kissed me and said, with deep feeling, "I do hope that you will not think of being married for a long time." Marriage to her was the end of a woman's independence.

After I grew up, as when I was younger, dances would have come very high in our list of favourite amusements, though I imagine that in these days they would be considered very stuffy affairs. Certainly etiquette held a tight rein over them. No man over the age of eighteen might go to a dance without tails and white kid gloves. I remember once going to a dance with Will. "I've forgotten my gloves." he said. We had to return to the house to fetch them. The ladies wore evening-dresses touching the ground and usually carried a fan, to be used between dances by her partner. Each lady was given a pink programme, each gentleman a blue, with the list of the dances and the name of the tunes, printed on it. Except at a big dance where a mother or other lady-chaperon was essential, a brother might escort a sister. It was not considered quite nice for a girl to dance more than twice with the same man. I did not always keep this rule, nor did I think it quite a perfect dance unless at least one man said I danced best in the room.

In my youth young people were far more dependent on their parents for their entertainment than they would submit to being nowadays. Girls whose names had just been added on their mother's visiting-cards, never went to a grown-up dance without a chaperon, even at a friend's house. And it would not have occurred to her brothers to go, even for a walk in London, with one girl alone. In spite of these restrictions dances were great fun, particularly in private houses with large drawing-rooms. A girl's first object was to get her programme filled. If a girl did not seem to know many men a good hostess would introduce her to some. The supper-dances were the most important of all, because one usually danced all of them with the same partner, as well as having supper with him. It was tiresome if he happened to be very hungry, as that took too much time off from dancing. Suppers were substantial. There was usually a turkey stuffed with a whole tongue, and galantine of veal with pistachio-nuts and truffles, and trifles and jellies. Between dances there were ices and meringues. There were often cups of hot soup before facing the cold air in a four-wheeler. At a youthful party the drinks were usually claret-cup and lemonade. For dances in the Season the menus were more elaborate; often there were salmon and lobster, plovers' eggs in aspic, and great bowls of strawberries and cream. And there was champagne to drink. I remember a big dance given at Queen's Hall in aid of some hospital. Anthony Hope Hawkins was there, sitting in a large leather armchair. He spoke to no one. It was said that his silence was due to the fear that, if he spoke, he might use some priceless phrase which he might otherwise have put into a book. A specially good dance I remember was given by Mr. and Mrs. Walter Crane at their house in Holland Park, Kensington, for their son, Lionel's, twenty-first birthday. It was a fancy dress dance and the garden and tent for dancing were lit up by fairy lamps. I was surprised to see a few girls strolling about. smoking cigarettes like their partners. My mother, like the other older ladies, merely had her hair powdered. Irene and I were in different frocks after Walter Crane designs. I remember Walter Crane coming up to me and saying "Have you seen the Missus?" Alas, I had not seen her. I am glad to know that a plaque has been put on the house where Walter Crane lived.

But this absorption in the life of their daughters, sometimes long after they were grown-up, was often pushed to the verge of absurdity. I remember our housekeeper, Miss Martin, telling me that my mother had told her not to tell me that our bailiff's wife was expecting another baby. By then I must have been in my late teens. She was shocked when she discovered that a schoolboy grandson had been present at the birth of a calf.

As far as my memory supports me the question of Women's Suffrage did not become a burning one until the turn of the century. I remember that shortly before I left school a few of my friends talked of the need to get women to take more interest in matters that concerned women, such as hours of work and conditions under which they worked—which were often appalling—and child labour. Issues ignored by many men. The long delay in granting women the Parliamentary Vote was partly due to women themselves. There were different opinions about suitable applications for the vote. Unmarried women said that married women would only vote as their husbands told them or friction would be caused. Married women said they had as much right to it, and more, as they had their children's rights to think of. I listened to Lady Courtney and her sister, Miss Potter, (later Mrs. Philip Snowden) both ardent advocates of Women's Suffrage, and to my mother and her friends who were, not so much against it, as indifferent to it. I am ashamed to say that I took little interest in it, either way.

The Boer War, which began in 1898, was the last war in which England took part to be waged without modern weapons. There were no aeroplanes, no tanks. But the Boers produced superb marksmen. A nineteen year old cousin of mine, a Second Lieutenant in the Royal Welsh Fusiliers, was shot through the head when, contrary to express orders, he raised his head above the trench facing the enemy lines.

On Bonfire Night huge effigies of Kruger were burnt. Boys whistled and sang new versions of nursery rhymes against "Old Kruger" and the entire race of Boers. Kipling wrote a ballad called "The Absent-minded Beggar" which was aimed at getting money for "the girl he left behind him." It was poor verse but was recited in and out of season. I remember one of these occasions at a young peoples' dinner party given by Dr. and Mrs. Rutherford in Westminster. We were all chatting happily when a girl suddenly rose and recited the poem. Everyone looked uncomfortable, no one put his hand in his pocket to "give, give, give." Most of us had only enough money to pay our cab home.

There were many dissentient voices raised against the Boer War. Not only on the Continent where the anti-Boer War feeling was very strong, but in England, too. As the war at last began to turn in our favour, so the conscience of many told them that it was wrong for so great a nation to wage war against a small one. The *Daily Mail* supported them and lost a great numbers of its readers in consequence. The Misses Mary and Margaret Eve spent their spare time in making garments for the children, shut up with their mothers in camps established for them by our generals. Irene and I were in Paris before the Boer War ended and I remember that small boys called after us such expressions as "Voilà les Boères" suggesting, no doubt, that we should at once take to our heels. A different picture is shown by the relief of Ladysmith when London went wild. The news must have come in the evening, I was in bed. Suddenly a great volume of sound came from the direction of Bayswater Road. I had acute hearing in those days and could hear the tramp of merry feet and a confused babel of voices. Next morning I read that Ladysmith, which had been be-sieged by the Boers, had been relieved. All night the streets had been packed with people. Everyone in uniform had been carried shoulder high. But animosity between English and Dutch remained for a very long time. Friends of mine who had relatives in South Africa told me that the two nationalities seldom met socially. Both had their own tennis and other clubs. The wife of a judge in South Africa said that one day the wife of a Dutch judge called on her. They became good friends. After a while the English wife said to the other "You know I was rather surprised at your calling on me." "Oh," said the other, "it was just a mistake. I had got down the wrong number of your house. I should certainly not have called otherwise."

It was said that grief over the Boer War hastened Queen Victoria's death. I do not remember the date of the second tragedy. It was in Paris. The scene was a great Charity Bazaar. How a fire started in a temporary building erected for the Bazaar, no one seemed to know. Suddenly the cry "Fire" rang out. The building was full of ladies in flimsy muslin frocks. Everyone rushed for the few exits. Many were crushed or burnt to death. One young girl, stark-naked, was seen staggering just outside the blazing tent. A young footman saw his young mistress, clasped her in his arms and rushed with her to the waiting carriage. The impression made on me, a young girl, by the awful death of many other young girls, has never faded.

While I was growing up there was a wide gap between the professional or upper middle class and the lower middle class. To the former belonged bishops and other beneficed clergy, officers in Her Majesty's Forces, judges and barristers, solicitors only if of outstanding position. To these might be added merchants and stockbrokers if they had shown exceptional ability by amassing huge fortunes, and civil servants both at home and abroad and publishers. To the latter belonged all shopkeepers, except for a few whose wealth took them to the highest class in the land, farmers, except so-called gentleman-farmers who left all the hard work to their bailiffs, all clerics except those belonging to the Church of England. There were also the unclassified because unclassifiable, artists of all descriptions, painters, musicians, journalists, novelists and poets. This artificial division of Society into departments was not only a very stupid but an evil one. For one thing it gave a number of young people a feeling of quite misplaced importance and of superiority to others, which was unjustified, and to many others a deep feeling of dissatisfaction with their lot. I remember my mother telling me that she had asked a working man what he was complaining about, and he said, "I want to be like you".

We were all now at the stage when everyone wants to know what you are going to be? In my day that query only applied to boys.

Girls in my kind of society were expected to be content with what their parents provided them with. And judging by the lives of many of my acquaintances that was precious little. Many girls of my day suffered from having ill-educated mothers. Mothers whose sole education was derived from a governess with no qualifications beyond a lady-like appearance, often the daughter of the incumbent of a little country parish with a small income and a large family. This lady probably had the assistance of a music-master and her pupils also joined classes for drawing and French. But for many girls all education stopped at the age of seventeen or eighteen. Boys were another matter. Their education was both expensive and necessary. Many of their sisters seemed to lose the power of initiative and they would have been far happier had they been obliged to earn their living. As it was, they were dependent on their parents for the amenities of life. In some cases the mothers, having seen their daughters through childhood, thought their duty was done. And life became a rather dreary round of shopping in the morning and paying calls in the afternoon. I was eighteen when my mother took Irene and me to our first play. It was called 'Our Flat' and was an amusing account of a young couple who, to impress the young man's father, turned a number of packing cases into settees and chairs by means of a few yards of chintz. It did not seem odd to us that my mother went with us to choose the material for our party frocks, and then took us to her dressmaker to decide on the design of the dress and come with us at the 'fittings'. But in spite of these restrictions I am quite sure that neither Irene nor I felt we had any cause for complaint. Probably due to our High School education we were more alive to the need for wresting the best out of life for ourselves, than were many of the girls we knew. It was not long after I left school that uncle Tom offered me his fencing outfit. So I went back to Captain Chiozzo's Gymnasium and took lessons in fencing. They were quite amusing although I was not a very apt pupil. However the small knowledge of the skill I acquired enabled me to entertain several small boys of my acquaintance. Our large circle of relations, too, were a source of interest: we had over twenty first cousins and a vast number of second cousins. A convenient race, the latter, for, as my mother used to say, you were under no obligation to see more of them than you chose.

To return to my own family. Will had left Marlborough at seventeen. He was a late-developer with, so far, no decided tastes. When engineering was suggested to him he made no serious objections, so it was arranged for him to enter an engineering firm as a pupil. But first, my father thought that six months in the United States would give him a taste of independence. John Walter, proprietor of *The Times*, offered some introductions and he and Mrs. Walter invited Will to spend a weekend at Bearwood, their country house in Berkshire. Will delighted us with his account of that great house. It had a hundred bedrooms, most of them having a bathroom. There was a fleet of domestics, male and female, who dogged one's footsteps. Will's first introduction in the States was to a widow living in a fine apartment in New York. She received him very kindly. "You are just in time," she told him, "to come with me to visit my husband's grave. I go there every month and this is my day for going." The grave was in a beautiful setting of brilliant flowerbeds and avenues of fine trees. But the visit seemed a little incongruous as a boy's first introduction to a new country. Rather like beginning a dinner with dessert and ending it with soup. Mark had left Rugby without any great love for classics and as little but classics were taught in Rugby of his day he went up to Balliol to study law with a view to becoming a barrister. Unlike Will, who disliked all games, Mark delighted in them and was fairly good at both cricket and tennis. Soon after going to his preparatory school he asked, "Father, I know that W. G. Grace is a better cricketer than I am, but is he so very much better?" Unfortunately the great Master of Balliol College—Jowett—had died just before Mark went to up Oxford. My future husband, Edward McCurdy, was under Jowett for the last four years of the Master's life and told me several tales about him. Edward was reading history. Jowett asked him to come up for an interview and to have lunch with him. "What will you drink?" the Master asked him. "Port, please," he replied. Jowett turned to the butler, "Bring a bottle of port," he said.

Every week his undergraduates brought him an essay for his criticism. He did not mind if sportsmen introduced sport into their essays but he would not allow non-sportsmen to write about sport. Edward was once reading him an essay on Bunyan. As well as discussing the *Pilgrim's Progress* he went on to *The Holy War* also by Bunyan. Jowett stopped him. "Have you read it?" snapped Jowett. "Yes," Edward answered. "I haven't," said Jowett, "You can go on." One of Edward's friends came out of his essay reading looking very pleased with himself. "Well, what did he say?" "He said, if I worked hard I might improve." "He couldn't have said much less," said Edward. Jowett used sometimes to ask a few of the undergraduates to come in for a glass of wine after dinner to meet some of his guests. One evening Edward was one of the young men asked to meet Gladstone. He was sitting on a sofa next to

Miss Margot Tennant. And that was as much as any of the under-graduates saw of Gladstone. An invitation to drink wine or to come to breakfast was tantamount to a Royal Command. An invitation to breakfast was once disobeyed. A scout brought a note to the Master's Lodgings, "Prince Chittiboo" (I cannot remember the correct name) "presents his compliments to the Master and regrets that as it is so cold he is staying in bed."

While Mark was up at Balliol Irene and I spent several delightful weeks at Abingdon during Eights Weeks. We used to drive over to Oxford in our hostess's pony-cart, have lunch at Buol's in the High, then watch the races from the Balliol barge. Compton Mackenzie sometimes joined the party on the Balliol barge and was, we thought, a little too forward on a barge which did not belong to his own college. I remember his acting as a bus conductor and demanding, "All fares please". After supper came the five mile drive back to Abingdon along a great avenue of trees, their top-most branches almost meeting over-head, so as to shut out, intermittently, the light of the moon, while the singing of rival nightingales kept us drowsily awake.

One of Irene's chief interests was drawing. When she left school she entered the Slade School in Gower Street. She spent some time drawing from casts of Greek and Roman sculpture, always longing for the time when she would join the Life class. The chief instructors were Professor Tonks, and the figure and landscape artist, Wilson Steer. Will Rothenstein and William Orpen were students at the Slade at the same time as Irene. Some of the pupils were boys of about fifteen who had had so little schooling that they could scarcely read and write: so a rule was made that no student should be admitted unless he or she had passed an elementary examination on General Knowledge. Irene told us of some of the models. One was a young Negro. One of the students spoke of him as a nigger. "Not Nigger—Negro," said the young man.

Irene was very pretty and attractive, but not at all strong. Many outings were spoilt for her by a headache before the end of the day. She married Clement Du Pontet, a classical master at Harrow. He had been in love with her since she was twelve years old. Irene died when their son was six and their little girl was just going to be four years old. A doll's pram had been promised for her birthday and the child in-sisted that it should be put outside the nursery window so that Mummy might see it.

Nigel's career was settled for him just as he was finishing his time at St. Andrew's University. This was in 1899 and the Boers had just declared war on Great Britain. The War Office were offering commissions in the Royal Engineers and the Royal Artillery to University graduates. Two were allotted to St. Andrew's. Nigel applied for one of these and was successful. He was appointed to the Field Artillery. He would have preferred the Horse Artillery but my father was unwilling to allow him the £300 a year, beyond his pay, which would have been necessary in the Horse Artillery. The war was over before Nigel's training was completed and he was sent to India. I remember well his first leave. He must have had a happy time during the voyage home. As an elderly lady passenger put it: "he was at the age when you did not know whether to offer him a chocolate or a cigarette". On his way over he had planned his first meal in London. It was to be at the Trocadero and he would take Mark and his new American wife, and me—Irene must have been away at the time. We should start with whitebait, then roast pheasant and some sort of iced sweet would finish the meal. I remember that Nigel was disappointed when Mark shared a hansom with his wife—Nigel thought he might have left her to him. But Mark thought otherwise.

Nigel had always been a somewhat puckish boy. He and a friend of his, the red-haired Gosse boy, son of Edmund Gosse, the producer of the many-coloured Christmas story books, might be seen hanging on to the tails of carts, while the driver, urged on by other small boys to "whip behind Mister" tried in vain to dislodge them. Another trick was to run down area steps, ring the backdoor bell and run back before the cook could open the door. One morning the cook was ready for them: out she bounced, frying pan in hand, after them up the area steps. Fat as she was she would have caught them but her breath gave out. Then there were the Saturday mornings with the Board School boys in what Nigel told us, Mr. Wilkinson's boys called Caddyboys' Lane.

6   *A Very Happy Family*

That leaves myself to deal with as best I may. I feel that I must have been rather a puzzle to a Victorian family. I was so full of energy and never content to sit at home doing the things that normal girls did. But then I had no parlour tricks that might have served to fill out my day: I could not draw well, and I could not play the piano nor sing. I was, in spite of my defects, a good deal spoilt by my parents. My mother, though far more talented than I, but who had only received the normal education for young ladies of her day, thought me clever. My father was pleased when his friends told him they enjoyed talking to me. He spoke of me sometimes as the head of the family, which must have been very galling to my brothers—if they heard it. In spite of all this eulogy I have little to show beyond a few bindings, a slight account of a rather remarkable set of aunts, and a fine set of my own offspring, which will, I hope, re-establish the McCurdy family.

In my early twenties interests came thick and fast upon me. I belonged to two small Societies. The first was the 'Seekers', with Professor W. P. Ker as our President. He was Professor of English at University College, London and a Fellow of All Souls. He was a very silent man but that gave us all the more chance of talking ourselves. The two delightful young men, Teddy Byrne, son of Mr. Justice Byrne, and Maurice Webb, son of Sir Aston Webb, a well-known architect of his day, were both killed in the First World War. These two made the rules and chose the members. One rule was that no male member should be allowed to marry a female member. The idea being, I believe, that we should be a family, not a match-making concern. Two of the girl members were Elska Ramsay, daughter of Sir William Ramsay, the scientist, and Elsie Brunton, daughter of Sir Lauder Brunton, a fashionable physician of his day. We met in one another's houses and ended the meetings with refreshments provided

63

by our mothers. We discussed many subjects, some suggested by Professor Ker, some by ourselves, Once, I remember, we turned a scene from Hamlet into modern prose. One summer our President entertained us on the All Soul's barge for the Henley Regatta. We returned by inviting him to dinner at a Soho restaurant, followed by a visit to a music hall. My first visit to such an unheard-of place. Professor Ker was not married but satisfied his love for young people by having several 'adopted nieces'. It was while travelling in Switzerland with two of them that he met his death. It was on a mountain pass. He was in front with one of two nieces he had taken for a Swiss holiday. He turned to see that the other girl was all right. He fell and died.

The other Society was called 'The Society for the Prevention of Quiet Evenings'. It was started by two young men, Lucius Oldershaw and Bernard Longden-Davies, both old Paulines, who had opened a school at Burgh Heath for boys, who for some reason or another had been misfits at their public schools. These two men, and G. K. Chesterton, had married sisters. All wrote articles for *The New Statesman*. As soon as a new number came out the three girls would rush to their mother, new issue in hand. "Mother you must read this article"—by Gilbert or Lucius or Bernard—"there's nothing else in the paper worth looking at". These Meetings, too, were held at one another's houses. But here the likeness ended. Where, under the chairmanship of our beloved Professor Ker, we were none of us afraid to voice our opinions, at the S.P.Q.E. Meetings many of us merely listened to the brilliant talk of our leaders. G. K. Chesterton stayed at his brothers-in-law's school and was very amusing. He never had children of his own but he was devoted to the Oldershaw family. The school was very expensive to run. I remember Mrs. Oldershaw telling me that one day Gilbert Chesterton cheered her up by assuring her that Father Brown was not dead yet. I often went over to the school as it was a pleasant bicycle ride from Walton. Once there was a fancy dress dance there. I remember it chiefly because I only thought next day of the answer I should have given to a remark of Chesterton's. I was standing waiting for the carriage to drive me home. "Do sit down," he said. "It's not worth while," I answered. "How like a woman", he said. To which I should have said, "Being a woman how else would you expect me to behave?" But the right answer never comes till next day. Chesterton had a great dislike of cyclists. He said that when he saw one coming along a country road he stood still with his umbrella stretched full length across his chest. I wonder what he would have thought of the hosts of motor-cars?

It was in 1899 that bookbinding became one of the main interests of my life. Mrs. Rutherford, wife of the Headmaster of Westminster, was calling on my mother one Tuesday afternoon. "I started bookbinding," she told me, "but I found it took too much time so I gave it up. I wonder whether you would care to have my plant? It is very fascinating." I thought I would and she sent it to me. I went for some lessons to a little room in the Albert Hall. It was one of a number of similar rooms all round the Albert Hall, behind the Galleries. It was a pleasant little lady who taught me. But, as she said, it was only the roughest type of binding that she taught—good enough for keeping together Tauchnitz editions that you like to keep. She told me of a Miss Ashbee who taught bookbinding in Cheyne Walk, Chelsea. She, too, I liked but she was not a very good binder and by this time I was in love with the craft. I do not remember how I heard of Douglas Cockerell but I do remember my first meeting with him. I asked him if he would take me as a pupil for six months. He said he was not sure. I said, "You must think of me as well as of yourself." Rather an odd way of putting it, perhaps, but he said he'd take me. So began a wonderfully happy six months for me.

The bindery was in a narrow little street, off Museum Street, up a rickety stairway. There was a sort of cloakroom where the men and girls left their coats, and beyond it, though I never penetrated so far, a lavatory. This I discovered one day when a friend visited me and— to my acute embarrassment—asked to retire. There were two men, Sangorski and Sutcliff, who did the binding under Mr. Cockerell's supervision, and two girls who did the sewing and mending. They were a delightfully friendly group. All Londoners, except the younger girl who came from Edinburgh, and was astonished when I called Edinburgh a lovely city. There were two other pupils, besides myself. Annie Power, the ninth and youngest child of an oculist, and Audrey Ricketts, whose chief reason for learning to bind books was because her stepmother wished to remove a rather disturbing element from the family circle. Her father, a Territorial Colonel, had married as his second wife, a strict member of the Society of Christian Scientists. I stayed once with the Ricketts family in a lovely old house called Boys Hall. Mrs. Ricketts used to read a chapter of what she obviously thought was a superior version of the Bible, to the family, except her husband, every day after breakfast. On the Sunday, when the Colonel and his wife had retired, as usual, to their own sitting room, after supper, we younger ones thought a game of whist would be fun. We were in the middle of a rubber when the door was flung open—we must have laughed too loudly—Mrs. Ricketts advanced to the table, snatched up the cards, and said "You know cards are not allowed on a Sunday," cast a withering look at me and swept out of the room.

Annie Power's family were of that magnificent Yorkshire type, big of bone and independent of spirit, that finds all men equal. Woe betide a visitor to such a place as Whitby if he show a different attitude. The Powers had owned for generations a large, dark, diamond-paned house on the outskirts of the town. When I stayed with them there were two unmarried, two married daughters, a son-in-law, five grandchildren and a nurse in the house. To give Dr. and Mrs. Power a breathing space, most of us spent the day on the moors. We ate a huge bap and a stick of chocolate in the middle of the day, filling up with a true Yorkshire tea before returning to dinner. It was the custom of the grandfather, with one or two of the younger members of the family, to stroll down to the sea and watch the waves breaking along the coast, from the pier. The wall at the end of the pier was broken at intervals to provide resting places. One evening, as usual, Dr. Power stood at the end of the pier while his daughter, Lucy, aged about twenty-four and his granddaughter, Lucy, a few years younger, sat in an embrasure in front of him. Suddenly a huge wave rose above the pier and, as it retreated, swept the two girls back with it. The father, the grandfather, was helpless. No one could have survived in that boiling sea.

To return to the bindery. The two men and the girls were all cityborn and bred. But they all liked to hear country talk. Over our four o'clock break for tea Douglas and I compared notes on birds and flowers, and it seemed to open a new world to them. I found the two men very interesting to talk to though their views were rather narrow. I asked them once whether women ever did the actual binding: "Oh no," they said, "we don't let women do the binding." "What about us?" I asked. "Oh, we don't mind you," they said, "You pay a lot for learning. But we won't let our women do the binding." I remember Sutcliff once telling me that Sangorski was engaged to be married. "The girl," he said, "is a parson's daughter. And he's in love with her, the way you'll be in love. Not the way we are. We marry for all sorts of reasons. Because we're tired of living at home. Because we want young'uns: because we've got a girl in trouble and 'er dad insists on it. All sorts of reasons but we don't just fall in love, just like that." Later I heard that the two men had set up in a bindery of their own and were doing very well. That was after Douglas and his wife had moved to Ewell, in Surrey, and were working there. Here, in a charming old cottage, their first child was born. A lovely little daughter. And here our dear old parlourmaid, Mrs. Felix, cooked for them. And as often as I decently could, I bicycled over to lunch with them. I lost sight of the two girls, but I always remember with gratitude that one of them gave up a good deal of her spare time to mend a book which had been given me to bind and had been accidentally torn.

After my six months were up Annie Power and I proposed to share a workshop together. This we found in Museum Street, a large first floor room with two good windows. Highly excited by the prospect I told my parents what I proposed to do. "Out of the question," said my father. "What would our friends say if they saw you going off like that." I burst into tears and retired to bed. Next morning I had breakfast with Irene, then working at the Slade School, at eight o'clock. At eight-thirty I left the house for Museum Street, a distance of about two miles. And that was the last I ever heard of my father's objections. And to do both my parents due credit, they remained the most affectionate and charming parents that a rebellious daughter could have desired.

While Annie and I were working in Museum Street, where she had a pupil to add to her sparse income, a girl came in to ask if she might have a few lessons in binding old books of music. A long willowy girl with a lovely Madonna-like face. She was Virginia Stephen, Sir Leslie Stephen's youngest daughter. At this period she was spending much of her time studying Greek with a woman classical scholar, a Miss Case, who lived in Hampstead. For anyone wishing to write, her father told her, Greek literature was a better guide than Latin. When Annie Power left to join Mr. Ashbee's group of craftsmen in Chipping Campden and I moved to Queen's Road—now Queensway—Bayswater, Virginia joined me there whenever she chose to come. Both she and her sister, Vanessa, used the workshop as an amusing place in which to pass a few hours and I became a fairly close friend of theirs. In dress Virginia never followed the fashions. I remember her in close-fitting, light grey dresses with none of the chains and bangles so profusely used in those days. At a young people's dinner-party at my home I remember her saying that all girls should dress for dinner in tight-fitting blue silk dresses. Burne-Jones would have agreed with her. Alas! we do not all have figures to match.

My life at the turn of the century was full of interest. All through the summer there were weekend guests, and tennis parties. All very pleasant for us, but what a burden for my mother. The big London house had been given up, but as my father was a true Londoner at heart there was a flat near Bryanston Square. And most of the domestic arrangements fell to her lot. True she had a housekeeper—our dear Miss Martin—but delightful as she was throughout her thirty years' service with us until the death of my parents, most of the brainwork fell to my mother. She used to say that Miss Martin's suggestions for a suitable meal for a small luncheon-party seldom went beyond a roast chicken and a nice apple-tart. It was my mother, too, who saw the bailiff every week and paid his staff and talked over farm matters. So, too, with the head-gardener. It was she who planned the new rock-garden and the filling of the flower-beds. Besides all this she was as excited as ever over the finding of a flower that she had not yet painted. When there were no more to be found, she began to paint grasses and finally fir-cones. In her younger days she had possessed a lovely soprano voice, trained by the organist of St. George's, Windsor. These gifts of his wife were much appreciated by my father, all of whose fingers were thumbs and who never sang a note in his life. But it appeared to us children though never, I am sure, to my mother, that he took his wife's devotion rather for granted. But perhaps for those days this judgement is a little unfair. Was not the male born to rule, the female to be his willing slave? Did not nurses, and in my youth every family had a nurse, treat the boys as superior beings? Were not the sons supplied with expensive tutors and public schools, while the daughters' education was left to the hands of inadequately trained governesses and to finishing schools at home or abroad, where most of the attention was paid to deportment and strumming of the piano, and where the art classes consisted in copying water-colour sketches produced by the art master. But if the education of young ladies left much to be desired, what of that provided for the female young on whom depended so much of the comfort of the wealthier classes. There were Board Schools and Infant Schools. But in the country districts these were often staffed by men and women who had had little education themselves. The boys at thirteen followed their fathers into the fields and gardens. And the girls, at the same age, took jobs as kitchen-maids or under-housemaids in the big houses in the neighbourhood or ventured further afield. If the boys were intelligent and ambitious they soon sought work in the towns. But the girls met with many restrictions. Many trades were not open to women. Of those that were I have first-hand knowledge of two: upholstery and bookbinding. I have dealt with the second already and I have also reliable knowledge of the first. I can see her now, broad-beamed, black-haired, red-cheeked, Miss Stacey. Snipping away at the shiny chintz which was to cover our drawing-room sofas and chairs to keep their satin covers clean for party use. It was always chintz, not cretonne in those days and the patterns were small and neat, not bold and sprawling. And as she worked Miss Stacey told us how her father, having no son, had secretly taught her his trade. A trade that no women might enter. I do not know how my mother heard of her. But I should guess that it was through some dealer in china and antique furniture, called Morgan, who had a shop in Soho. The sort of shop that my mother loved. I remember the dealer and his sister, well. They had known all the big dealers but had not had their flair for business.

Looking back on my childhood after so many years some anomalies strike me. My parents were intelligent, devoted and well-to-do. Yet they left the education of my sister and me in the hands of a young woman whose only qualification for the post was that she had gained a Certificate from the College of Preceptors. As well as the three Rs she taught us to play the piano. My mother said that as she passed the schoolroom door she heard the same wrong notes played day after day. Yet she, who had been her singing master's favourite pupil, did not provide us with a better teacher. She and my father went, season after season, to the Saturday afternoon Concerts at Queen's Hall—called the Saturday Pops—yet our musical training was entirely neglected.

In our circle I do not think that the mistress of the house did much personal shopping. The butcher's boy, the grocer's boy, the milk float pushed along by sturdy Welsh girls, called for orders every day and delivered them shortly. But on a Saturday morning we often went to Whiteley's in Queen's Road and bought food for our own consumption. We could choose any biscuits at fivepence halfpenny a pound—a large assortment such as Garibaldi, Osborne and ginger-nuts. And penny buns at seven for sixpence. Everything at Whiteley's was slightly cheaper than anywhere else. It was said that he paid lower wages than any other shop-keeper but as he never required a reference this was accepted. I have often seen Mr. Whiteley himself in his shop. A stout man in a grey frock coat and a topper. He lived in a large house with fine stables in Porchester Terrace. He had risen from a life of poverty and by sheer hard work had built up a flourishing business. His end was tragic. He was shot in his own shop by a man who declared that Mr. Whiteley had seduced and deserted his mother. He claimed to be Mr. Whiteley's son.

So much is written about the harsh treatment and narrow existence of Victorian children that a Victorian child who passed and remembers a very happy childhood, owes it to her parents, teachers and domestics to say a few words in their defence. We were born, probably, at the parting of the ways, between the period when children were looked on as creatures so apt to break out in so many undesirable directions unless actively checked, that the methods to restrain them were often akin to those applied in topiary art; and the period when the little darlings were so pampered that they became unbearable, as typified by the American children met with in European hotels. Better education for girls had a good deal to do with the more rational treatment of both girls and boys. The time had passed when a girl spent her days in practising at the piano or making samplers. But there were still far too many girls, who without any guidance, spent much of their lives in reading trashy novels and merely passing the time. Two of my greatest friends were entirely governess-taught. One by what may be called a governess of all work and the other by English, French and German governesses. In both cases their brothers went to public schools and afterwards to Oxford or Cambridge. This difference of treatment was not meanness nor indifference. It was a lingering feeling that in matters of the intellect a woman should leave it to the male.

I sometimes wonder whether one of the reasons for so many broken marriages in these days is the emancipation of women. I have heard many young men ask why they should give up their seats to girls, and in many ways make concessions to their sex, when women claim equality in all ways with men. In my youth the father was, certainly in most families, the dominant figure and his wife was content to play second fiddle. He was the talker, she the listener. If his audience were female, this is how they desired it. Though, indeed, I knew a delightful couple where the husband declared he enjoyed listening to his wife's clever talk. But, as they were both middle-aged when they married, they are not typical. Young people in these days have so many opportunities of getting to know one another that they cannot plead ignorance of each other as they certainly could in my parent's day. I remember my father telling me that after he was engaged to be married to my mother he scarcely ever went out with her unaccompanied by one of his sisters. Playing gooseberry, as it was called. On the rare occasions when they were out alone together he would put her into a four-wheeler, giving the cabman instructions to put her down further along the street, in case her father should see her. How then is it that with all the advantages young people have of getting to know one another before marriage, divorces are frequent. Is it, perhaps, because in these days of excessive speed young people hanker for a change of partner asthey do for a bigger and faster motorcar.

One summer after Annie Power had joined Mr. Ashbee's group of craftsmen at Chipping Campden she invited me to spend a few weeks with her. Although by this time I had achieved a certain amount of freedom—in the day-time Irene and I were no longer accompanied by our maid—yet we knew nothing of working class housekeeping. My visit to Annie opened my eyes to some of the limitations forced upon them by want of money. Wages, even for highly skilled craftsmen, were very low and, since there were no electrical gadgets, women's domestic work was hard. I had supper with a delightful couple with two small boys and was astonished when Annie told me that the tongue I was given—and it was not offered to the boys—must have been bought in my honour as it was beyond their means. The cottage we lived in consisted of two rooms, one above the other. There must have been a lavatory, there was certainly no bathroom. We did the minimum of housework and cooking. I once made an apple-charlotte but Annie said that but for the sound of the thing, she would as well eat apples and bread and butter. I did a little bookbinding but spent a good deal of time on a grassy hill just beyond the village, practising golf shots with a driver, as I had promised James Braid, our professional at Walton Heath, that I would do. We spent some evenings at the Ashbees' beautiful house where they invited the young craftsmen to sing part-songs and madrigals. Here I met William de Morgan and his wife. I do not think he was writing novels at this period, but designing tiles. I was particularly interested in tiles as my mother was designing and painting them. I had gone with her to a little factory in Soho to have them baked. Annie and I breakfasted very early and Mr. de Morgan came round for a chat before his breakfast was ready. Best of all were the week-ends. We would start off on our bicycles soon after breakfast —Annie had a theory that unmade beds were healthier than made beds to get into at night. In this way we visited Warwick. Here, in the grounds of Warwick Castle we saw a performance of *Alice through the Looking Glass*. If only the producer of the modern version could have seen what we saw, they would not have been guilty of the mis-cast, mis-understood monstrosity called 'Alice' I saw on the B.B.C. At Cumnor Place we saw and shuddered at the hole in the stair-case down which Amy Robsart fell to her death. Another week-end we went to Stratford-on-Avon, but there were no plays on then. After our sight-seeing we would find a simple lodging above a baker's shop before returning on Sunday to Chipping Campden. It was hot work cycling up the hills with the gnats busy at our arms and faces but downhill we soon outpaced them.

Soon after I left Douglas Cockerell and was ready to set up on my own, a well-known woman bookbinder offered me a job—I was, of course, to do the less interesting parts of the work, no pattern-making, no tooling, both of which I loved. She would give me, to begin with, sixpence an hour. I declined the offer. After I moved to Queen's Road my father no longer disapproved of my chosen occupation. In fact both my father and my mother took the greatest interest in it. My mother had always liked the idea of a handicraft. She was so clever herself at flower-painting and took so much interest in other people's work that she could not fail to be pleased when I became absorbed in bookbinding and my sister, Irene, in painting. Sometimes my parents came to tea with me and examined all I was working at. They were both delighted when friends gave me work to do and particularly pleased when I told them I had sold a couple of books to Mr. Baines, the bookseller, then in Charles Street, off the Haymarket. What a charming old-world character he was. He took me sometimes into the large room over the shop, where he used to feed the birds on the window-sills and talk about the literary people he had known. He did not like the S.S. I always signed my bindings with. He said it might be 'Sarah Smith'. But though I respected his judgement in other things, I did not alter my S.S., with 19 on one side and the year of the century on the other. Among those of my bindings I have with me, most are those books I bound for my mother of my father's published works. The earliest date is 1900.

During the spring and autumn we all spent most week-ends at Frith Park, very often with week-end visitors. In the Season there were dances and various outings and dinner-parties. Irene and I much enjoyed the days we spent at Abingdon with Mr. and Mrs. Reynolds. Mr. Reynolds had been for many years Rector of East Ham and had retired to a charming old house with a formal box-edged garden at Abingdon. The garden led down to a meadow where rooks built their nests in tall elms. In the late spring, year after year, men shot through the bottom of the nests and their wives made rookie pies of the fledglings that fell from the nests. Mr. Reynolds had been a Fellow of Brasenose and, in spite of his immense girth, still liked to act as an irresponsible undergraduate. When the passengers from Oxford to Abingdon changed trains at Radley and the old guard on the branch line called for tickets, Mr. Reynolds felt in every pocket but the right one, while the guard fumed at the delay. Mrs. Reynolds said "Oh! Harvey, Harvey, Harvey," and we young ones giggled. Sometimes we stayed in Oxford with Dr. and Mrs. Henry Daniel. At first when Dr. Daniel was Bursar of Worcester College, where my father had been a Scholar and a Fellow, and later when Dr. Daniel was Provost of that College. His two amusing little daughters, Rachel and Ruth, were children then. They had a page-boy, Arthur, who became a Scout at the College. When he was about sixteen Ruth said to him, "I suppose you call yourself a man now, Arthur?" His answer was, "I think, Miss Ruth, I am what is called a youth."

One of the changes that have taken place in my life-time is the disappearance of both indoor and outdoor domestic help. To the younger generation it appears rather shocking that we of my generation should have taken it for granted that many of the sons and daughters of the so-called lower class should spend their lives in tasks that we did not like to do for ourselves. They certainly added much to the comfort of our lives and many became our close friends. Conditions of service varied greatly. In some houses indoor domestics remained for many years and the posts of gardener or coachman passed from father to son. In other cases living conditions were very poor and some masters and mistresses were harsh and overbearing. In days when it was easy to go to a Registry Office and engage another servant, many were dismissed for trifles. I heard of a kitchen-maid of fifteen whose mistress told her to pack her box and leave the house at once, without a character, because on the previous day she had dared to play a tune on the drawing-room piano while her master and mistress were at church. Without a character written by the mistress, it was difficult for a domestic to get another post.

The rules for the behaviour of servants in fashionable and professional society were so strict that means had to be found to evade them. One such was the holding of dances in a nearby public house. I remember hearing a tune softly played after ten o'clock at night, passing from the top of one area steps to the next, and being told by Jane, our maid, that this was the sign for the men-servants and upper maidservants to attend a dance. Upper servants were often very tyrannical to the under-maids. My mother told me that the kitchen-maid once came up to her in tears. The cook, she said, had called her a "hussie". "Don't let that worry you", said my mother, "I am the only hussie in this house. It means housewife." In many houses visitors to the servants were strictly forbidden. And in many others permission had to be obtained from the mistress before any visitor, below stairs, was admitted. There was very little "time off" allowed, alternate Sunday morning off or afternoon from about 3 to 10 p.m. and a half-day during the week. The mistress insisted on morning tea being brought up to her at 7 a.m. so as to ensure that the work of the house began in good time. There were no easy methods of getting hot water. The kitchen fire had to be lighted in time to get sufficient hot water to fill the brass cans which were then carried up from the basement to the bedrooms on the second and third floors. These had to be large enough to fill the small baths placed ready in both bedroom and dressing-room for guests, who were not expected to share the one bathroom with the family. Even in a house as large as Frith Park there was only one bathroom until my mother had a second put on the back-stairs for the use of the maids and the visiting grandchildren.

Epilogue

In the course of my long life I have noted many changes. Some have been mere trifles, such as the alterations in fashions. When I was a girl women's dresses touched the ground, their edges protected by braid sewn to the material. As all the carriages and tradesmen's carts were horse-drawn, the streets were muddy and the skirt had to be lifted when crossing the road, but not far enough to expose the leg above the ankle. In the residential west end of London a crossing-sweeper would often establish himself and the residents would be glad to pay him small sums for the sake of having clean boots and unsoiled skirts. I remember a forbidding looking man with a patch over one eye, who arrived one day on our crossing, but the police gave him a good character as an ex-Crimean war veteran. Then, too, the position of women in the home has changed. No man would sit if a woman stood, and a man would always open a door for a woman. A gentleman did not swear when a lady was present, nor was sex mentioned in mixed society. Another forbidden subject was a woman's age. I remember a young man at our house asking an elderly lady whether she remembered some incident. She answered, indignantly, that she could not possibly remember it. She said to my father later, "But I did remember it, Mr. Stebbing!" But the really great change is that in the lives of the working class. I have never forgotten the sight of those pale, ragged little children, begging for pennies in Seven Dials, more than eighty years ago. After the Second World War, too, I saw ragged children in London, but never now. The well-fed, well-dressed, alert-looking children I see in London now-a-days promise well for the future of Great Britain. How great has been the change is evident from the accounts given me by three friends of mine, all now over ninety, of their lives when young. I am sure that their testimony is true. The first was left a widow with three young children. As she had no-one with whom to leave her children, all under school age, she earned a meagre living by doing odd jobs for her neighbours whose husbands were in regular work. As the poor are always kind to those who are worse off than themselves, they would get her to mind the baby while they took another child to the Parish Doctor, or gave her some washing to do. For these jobs she would get fourpence or fivepence. "And glad to get it". The second was a deserted wife. Her husband left her just after the birth of their eighth child. This baby soon died but she brought the rest up almost entirely by her own hard work, and they have turned out a credit to her. Every morning, except Sunday, she left the house, walked across the river and did office-cleaning from 6 to 7 a.m. And again from 6 to 7 p.m. for 25 shillings a week. She was a regular church-goer and the clergy, badly paid themselves, would help by passing on out-grown children's clothing from some of their better-off parishioners. My third friend was in a very different position to the other two, but it was still a struggle to make ends meet. She was one of a family of eleven children, seven daughters and four sons. Their father was a postman earning 25s. a week. In his off-times he did painting and paper-hanging for people in the bigger houses in Fulham. They themselves lived in a house, one up and one down, in one of the slums which existed, cheek-by-jowl, with the fine houses and squares in all the best parts of London in those days. Their mother was a good cook and a devoted wife and mother. She always sent the children to bed with a bowl of hot soup made from bones and bacon-rinds and any odd scraps of vegetable she or the children could collect. Food was very cheap in those days and the local butcher would give a child enough scraps from the joints to make a big pudding, for a few pence, and even, at closing-time, a scrag of mutton. At Harrods tea-dust could be bought for sixpence a pound. Sugar cost a penny three-farthings a pound, and as bread was sold by weight there were always odd bits of bread over and even a few broken cakes and pastries, to put into a child's bag, when there was no food in the house and no money to buy any. One or two of the children would be sent to the Guardians— in other words, the Workhouse, and they would give an order to some shop to supply a certain amount of food. No money was ever given.

All the children slept in one bed; the boys at one end, the girls at the other. When all were supposed to be in bed the father would come up and count them. The eldest child was a girl. She had a young man and sometimes stole off to a Cinderella Dance. Her father waited up for her and as soon as she was in bed, went up and gave her a taste of his strap. Sometimes one of the others would call out, "You've hit the wrong one, Dad!" "We were a very happy family", my friend assured me. And I'm sure she was right.